Croner'
DISCIPLINE

Written and compiled by
Croner's Employment Law
Editorial Department

CRONER PUBLICATIONS LIMITED

Croner House, 173 Kingston Road,
New Malden, Surrey KT3 3SS

Telephone: 01-942 8966

Croner's Guide to DISCIPLINE

First Edition
February 1982

© Copyright ICU (UK) Ltd.

ISBN   0 900319 26 7

Contents

Introduction   1

Discipline and the Law   5

The Need for Discipline   15

The Role of the First Line Manager   21

Informal Action is Important   25

Formal Procedures   39

Practical Application   65

Summary   87

Index   89

Printed for the Publishers, Croner Publications Ltd.,
Croner House, 173 Kingston Road, New Malden, Surrey KT3 3SS by
Dorling Print Group Ltd.,

Introduction

A glance at a dictionary or Thesaurus can show that there is tremendous width of meaning in the word "discipline".

"Discipline" n. 1) (mental self-training) preparation, development, exercise, drilling, inculcation, training, regulation, self-discipline; 2) (a system of obedience) — Syn. conduct, regulation, drill, orderliness, restraint, limitation, curb, subordination to rules of conduct, indoctrination, brainwashing.

From the latter it is small wonder that when the word "discipline" is used in its "heavy" sense it is considered a dirty word! Perhaps it is only the supervisor or manager who hankers after the benevolent regulation of armed forces life who can feel entirely happy using the word and those disciplinarians of the classical mould must be a dying breed in companies nowadays. However, there are amongst the dictionary definitions several more positive meanings for discipline than those associated with punishment, retribution and rigid compliance with the rules. It is these positive elements that are of most interest to people who manage staff in commerce, industry and other organisations. If these aspects of constructive discipline are properly understood trouble can be headed off before it actually starts to become an intractable confrontation situation.

Orderliness

For instance, "orderliness": this is usually seen as a desirable requirement in any organised group both by those in decision-making positions as well as those less influentially placed. Experience tells us that there is no management more severely criticised by their subordinates than one that is disorganised, lacking in direction and "can't get it together". Orderliness is imposed by day to day rituals of work, i.e. the time of day during which work is to be performed, the routine in job tasks that follow one after another and the methodical steps in completing the individual job tasks that build up the expectation of orderliness in the lives of all working people.

1

One need only think of the unfortunate redundant employee who still takes his train to town every day, even though he has nowhere to work, to realise the persuasiveness of routine and the comfort it gives.

In achieving orderliness, getting the procedures right is an essential step so that matters of poor conduct, capability, etc., can be dealt with in the right sequence and handled consistently by those in authority. The procedures can be a prop, taking away the anxieties of dealing with a variety of circumstances which in most organisations only occur occasionally. A large part of this book goes into detail about the operation of in-company disciplinary procedures and, particularly, using them with sensitivity to obtain a positive result.

Rules of Conduct

Those imbued with libertarian ideas may blanch at the idea of imposing "rules of conduct" particularly when they are put into writing and are served up as "company rules". However, what they do not recognise is that all companies or organisations have accepted standards of behaviour from which individuals are not expected to depart. They are hardly ever written down or even spoken about but nevertheless they are there and are tangible to any new recruit to the organisation. These norms of conduct, dress, etc., can vary from department to department and from company to company; the "laissez faire" standards adopted by one contrasting sharply with the almost Victorian strictness of others. Sometimes it is the result of a particularly strong-minded individual (not always the person in charge) who helps to set departmental standards, especially for the new recruit.

It goes like this:

- Hilda doesn't like other people being late back from lunch because it is not fair to everyone (but particularly herself because she doesn't have a break and therefore has to answer all the telephones).

- Hilda sits and fumes in the corner making pointed remarks.

- No one, just no one, likes to offend Hilda! (This is confirmed by everyone else in the department — from personal experience!)

- Everyone in the department is usually prompt in returning from lunch and loudly apologises if they are unavoidably detained.
- So new recruit conforms to the norm.
- End of story.

Of course, some standards of behaviour develop which are not beneficial to the company or organisation, i.e. sleeping on the night shift or claiming unworked overtime as an accepted "turn a blind eye" practice. Such situations will need a management lead to establish new acceptable standards of behaviour.

From the informal setting of standards it is easy for organisations to graft on formal rules of conduct and, with the advent of modern legislation, there are good commonsense reasons for doing so.

The codification of "works rules" or company rules outlining accepted standards of behaviour is a sensitive matter because the rules have to reflect custom and practice and be presented in an acceptable manner. The advantages of such an exercise are described at length later in the book.

Codifying Company Rules

When starting the exercise of codifying rules for your organisation, it is certainly helpful to look at examples from other companies, but don't forget that every organisation is unique and there may be particular rules that have grown up over time on an informal basis, perhaps even in individual departments. It is a good idea to involve all managers and supervisors in discussing the informal rules that they have made in their areas of responsibility before preparing the first draft. They are in the best possible position to know exactly how seriously they have treated any breach of such informal rules. Consequently, it will be possible to rank these breaches into three categories:

- minor misconduct that merits a verbal reprimand or warning;
- more serious misconduct that will result in written warnings; and
- gross misconduct which will usually attract the ultimate penalty of dismissal.

3

It will be immediately apparent that different standards or degrees of laxity exist between first line managers and these discussions will considerably help to improve consistency throughout the organisation.

If company rules already exist there is nothing to lose — and a great deal of benefit to gain — by repeating the exercise periodically to review them in the light of changed managerial personnel, company policy and omissions that have become apparent since they were first prepared.

Remember also that in some circumstances it may be advisable for good business/commercial reasons to have different standards in different parts of the company. If this is the case it is absolutely essential that there is no doubt whatever in employees' minds as to which rules apply to them and, preferably, why the different standards have been adopted.

Discipline
and the Law

By way of introduction to this chapter, there are two main points that should be stressed. First of all, the law does not say that companies must have disciplinary rules or policies, let alone prescribe what sort of procedures companies should adopt. What it does do, though, is to say that if companies dismiss an employee on grounds of his misconduct, the dismissal will be unfair if the employer acted unreasonably in treating the misconduct as a sufficient reason for dismissal. This is backed up by a Code of Practice issued by the Advisory, Conciliation and Arbitration Service which sets out some ground rules on fairness and this applies to employers in much the same way as the Highway Code applies to motorists: breach of any of the Code's recommendations will have to be justified if an unfair dismissal claim goes to an industrial tribunal.

The second point is that the law does say that if you have disciplinary rules, then details of them must be notified to employees, either directly or by referring them to a reasonably accessible document which specifies the rules.

The purpose of this book is not to provide legal advice on disciplinary matters but, in order that you can carry out the "man-management" part of your job effectively and, as far as possible, keep you and your company from running into trouble with industrial tribunals, this chapter looks at the main legal requirements on disciplinary practice and policies. The way that you can best handle the practical aspects of maintaining reasonable standards of conduct, while taking into account the legal requirements, is dealt with fully in pages 65 to 86.

Unfair Dismissal

An employee who works for at least 16 hours a week and has 52 weeks' service with a company has the right not to be unfairly dismissed. If he works in a company that has fewer than 20 employees throughout his time with them and he didn't start his job before 1 October, 1980, then protection against unfair dismissal doesn't apply until he has been employed for 104 weeks. Part-time employees who work for at least eight but less than sixteen hours a week don't have this protection until they have been employed for five years (this is 5 × 52 weeks, not 5 calendar years).

People who are dismissed because of sex or race discrimination or because of trade union membership or activity gain protection against being unfairly dismissed as soon as they join a company, so if an employee with less than a year's service claimed that he was dismissed for one of those reasons, then it would be up to the employer to show that the dismissal was really on grounds of conduct or one of the other potentially "fair" reasons for dismissal.

There are five such fair reasons:
- capability or qualifications for the work employees are employed to do (this includes health);
- conduct;
- redundancy;
- continued employment would involve the employer or employee in breaking the law; or
- some other substantial reason justifying the dismissal of the employee.

Making a Claim

Any employee who is sacked, and has the necessary 52 weeks' service, has the right to make a claim to an industrial tribunal that he has been unfairly dismissed. He makes a claim on a special form (IT1) which he then sends to the Central Office of Industrial Tribunals. They will send a copy of his form plus a form for the employer's defence — Notice of Appearance (IT3) — to the employer. If the claim cannot be settled through conciliation (which normally involves the employer making a payment to the ex-employee, but without any admission that the dismissal was unfair) then a tribunal hearing will be arranged, normally within about six weeks, but the delay between making the claim and the hearing taking place can vary enormously.

If the case does go to an industrial tribunal, the employer has to prove that there was a fair reason for dismissal and then it is a question of whether it was reasonable to treat the employee's behaviour as a sufficient reason for dismissal: in other words, did the punishment fit the crime? The important point here will be the procedure that was followed before the dismissal. This is where the ACAS Code of Practice comes in as it sets out the sort of procedure that is considered to be reasonable.

The ACAS Code of Practice

The Code of Practice on Disciplinary Practice and Procedures in Employment was published by the Advisory, Conciliation and Arbitration Service in 1977. The foreword to the Code states:

> "A failure on the part of any person to observe any provision of a Code of Practice shall not of itself render him liable to any proceedings; but in any proceedings before an industrial tribunal . . . any Code of Practice issued under this section shall be admissible in evidence, and if . . . relevant to any question arising in the proceedings it shall be taken into account in determining that question (s.6(11), Employment Protection Act 1975)."

As the Code sets out the essential features of disciplinary procedures and recommendations as to how the procedure should be operated, it is a very important document. Copies of the Code can be obtained from HMSO, price 30p. If all the Code's recommendations are not followed, it doesn't mean that a dismissal will be automatically unfair, though. It will then be for the employer to show that his procedure was fair in the circumstances of that particular company, and the particular case.

For instance, very small companies are not expected to have the same sophisticated procedures as would probably be found in a big multi-national business. Similarly, the sort of procedure that applies to a senior executive will often be different from that applied to a shop floor worker. The essential point is that the company behaves in a reasonable manner. Examples of the sort of behaviour expected from companies in different circumstances and for various kinds of misconduct are given on page 65.

It is worth stressing here that the Code does not impose unreasonably high standards. It wasn't drafted in terms of the highest possible standard that companies could aim for. What it does do is to recommend the sort of practice that was being followed by the majority of companies even before the first legislation on unfair dismissal was introduced. It is a very useful document in that it sets out, in a straightforward way, commonsense rules for promoting order and fairness in the treatment of individuals.

What the Code Says

The main provisions of the Code relate to the essential features of the disciplinary procedure and the way it should be operated. The main points for the purposes of this book are that disciplinary procedures should:

- be in writing (this is dealt with below);
- specify to whom they apply — this seems to be commonsense but it isn't unusual to find some employees who are quite sure that the rules really don't apply to them;
- provide the right for employees to hear the case against them and have the right to give their side of the story — this is particularly the case when somebody is apparently caught red-handed! It may well be that they have a good reason. It may also be the case that misconduct is actually rooted in domestic or health problems so you will want to change your approach;
- give employees the right to be accompanied — it is important to establish in your own company whether this means that the employee can have somebody else to speak for him or whether the person accompanying him is only there to "hold his hand". Another important point to settle is whether there are any restrictions on who the accompanying person can be. For instance, do you really want someone to turn up with their solicitor in tow?;
- ensure that there is a thorough investigation — this is a very important point and it is the lack of investigation that is most likely to lead to an unfair dismissal finding by a tribunal. If necessary, employees can be suspended for a brief period while the investigation is carried out, but the suspension should always be on full pay.

If, after the investigation, it is necessary to take formal disciplinary action against an employee, the Code suggests that the following steps should be taken:

(a) In the case of minor offences, the employee should be given a formal oral warning or, if the issue is more serious, there should be a written warning and the employee should be advised that the warning constitutes the first formal stage of the procedure.

(b) Further misconduct might warrant a final written warning.

(c) The final step might be disciplinary transfer or suspension without pay (but only if these are allowed for by an express or implied term of the contract of employment), or dismissal.

The essential feature of warnings is that they should clearly spell out the nature of the misconduct, the improvement expected within a specified time and the consequences of failure to improve or further breaches of the rules — i.e. final written warning, dismissal, etc.

Your Role at the Tribunal

In larger companies, the personnel or industrial relations manager/director is likely to handle the company's case before the tribunal and in smaller companies a solicitor might be retained. However, in almost all companies you, as a supervisor or manager, are likely to have a crucial role to play as a witness. After all, you should be the person who first set the disciplinary procedure in motion, even if you were only actively involved in the early, informal stages, and you will be the person with the best knowledge of the employee, his conduct and the steps that were taken to improve his standards.

It is vital that you are in a position to give good, accurate evidence: not only will your company's defence at the tribunal depend on that in many cases, but so will your credibility with both your subordinates and the people above you in the organisation. Your success as a witness doesn't depend on any intrinsic qualities, such as a talent for public speaking — or even acting! It will be a question of the way you handled the situation and the records you kept, and these points are dealt with in detail in later chapters of this book.

Putting it into Writing

The Employment Protection (Consolidation) Act 1978 says that all employees must be notified of any disciplinary rules that apply to them; either by giving them copies or telling them where they can be seen — in the personnel department, the supervisor's office, on company noticeboards, and so on — and, in the same way, they must be informed of who they can appeal to if they are dissatisfied with a disciplinary decision and how the appeal should be made.

It obviously makes a good deal of sense to have the rules and procedures in writing. It means that you know exactly what steps you can take, employees know where they stand, and union officials are better equipped to carry out their role. Written rules narrow any area of dispute and, if you've got to pull somebody up for bad timekeeping, horseplay or whatever, you don't want to get imbroiled in an argument as to what the rules or procedures say or mean!

The best way of ensuring that employees are left in no doubt as to the meaning of rules and the standards expected of them is to incorporate this into the induction procedure which each new recruit to the company should go through, and ensure at this stage that they either have their own copies or know where to go to refresh their memories.

What Rules?

The rules set for employees in your company will depend on your particular circumstances and no one set of rules can ever be right for every organisation. There are, though, some good ground rules which are helpful, one of which is that, as far as possible the rules should be positive: don't keep saying "you must not . . .", say "you will . . .".

The conduct required of every employee has the elements of good citizenship like those found in any community. These requirements take on a special significance at work. The company's financial stability, reputation, ability to offer employment security and the provision of safe working conditions depends on each employee's individual performance.

An example of the sort of rules most likely to be found in companies is given below.

Sample Rules

1.   You are required to be punctual in observance of times of work:

- you are required to report punctually for work at the time stated in your terms and conditions of employment (shift rota posted on the noticeboard, etc.);
- you must observe the stated luncheon and tea breaks;
- it is a requirement that you don't leave your workplace before the finishing time stated in your terms and conditions statement;
- your working times can only be varied with the written authority of your immediate supervisor;
- special conditions of attendance for (other categories of staff) are set out in the company procedural manual or statement of terms and conditions.

2. You are required to respect fellow employees:
- do not intimidate, threaten or coerce fellow employees by using physical violence, improper language or other disorderly conduct;
- maintain sanitary conditions in washrooms and keep your workplace tidy;
- do not distribute unauthorised pamphlets or literature;
- do not place unauthorised documents on the company noticeboard or remove or deface those documents placed with the authority of management;
- do not gamble on company premises;
- you must follow all reasonable instructions of supervisors and managers.

3. You are required to respect both the property of the company and your fellow employees:
- do not abuse, deface or wilfully damage company property;
- do not use company telephones for personal calls except in cases of emergency;
- do not accept personal telephone calls except in cases of emergency;
- company vehicles may only be used by authorised employees;
- use company property only for company activities. Do not take company property for personal use either on or off company premises;

- use your work time only for company responsibilities. Do not use work time for personal projects or for other time consuming activities.

4. You are required to protect personnel and company facilities:
- smoke only in those areas where smoking is permitted;
- do not carry any form of weapon, explosive or inflammable substance on the company premises;
- you are required to follow safe, normal work procedures and use only the equipment which you are authorised to use;
- always make sure that the safety guards provided are working correctly and are correctly positioned;
- in event of fire or other alarms follow standing instructions and the orders given by your supervisor or manager, immediately and in an orderly manner.

5. You are required to be free from the influence of alcohol or drugs:
- do not bring to the company premises intoxicating beverages or consume such beverages except in the case of organised occasions previously authorised by . . .;
- do not use, be under the influence of or bring to the company premises any form of narcotic other than those prescribed for your personal use by a registered physician.

6. You are required to be truthful and accurate when completing company documents and records:
- this requirement includes completion of all personnel forms, medical records, leave requests and other company forms;
- it is contrary to company rules under all circumstances to falsify the time or attendance records of a fellow employee or encourage a fellow employee to take such action on your behalf.

7. You are required to comply with the company's procedural handbook, copies of which can be seen on (company notice boards, in the supervisor's office, etc.):
- such written procedures which have a special effect on everyday life are circulated on a personal basis, e.g. such matters as those company instructions concerned with the operation of motor cars, employee expenses, holidays, pension, benefits, etc.;

- it is the responsibility of each employee to be aware of the contents of such procedures which might affect their working conditions.

8. You are required to keep information acquired during the course of your job in confidence:

- do not convey to any person not in the company's employ any document relating to the business of the company except those published for distribution to the general public;
- do not fill in or discuss any trading, marketing or financial surveys of any nature unless authorised in writing by a director of the company;
- do not disclose information concerning company products, product development or development plans except that which is published for circulation to the general public;
- do not discuss or disclose any matters concerning financial operations or trading practices to any unauthorised person within the company or to persons outside the company.

Breaches of these requirements will be dealt with under the company's disciplinary procedure as the circumstances require.

Common Law

Another aspect of the law to be taken into account is "common law" — that is, judge-made law rather than Acts of Parliament. For the purposes of this book, it is common law as it relates to contracts of employment. An employer who breaks an important term of an employee's contract will be in fundamental breach of the contract and the employee would be entitled to leave — with or without notice — and, providing he had the necessary qualifying service, make a claim to an industrial tribunal of constructive (unfair) dismissal. Alternatively, the employee could remain in his job but claim damages from the county courts in respect of the employer's breach.

Contractual Rules and Procedures

On page 9 we mentioned the importance of having the rules and procedures in writing and ensuring that copies are given to

13

all employees. Some employers do this by incorporating them into the contract of employment. This is fair enough in many ways but there are two potential problem areas:

- unless the full procedure is used for new employees who do not come up to standard, when they are dismissed they could get damages from the county courts for the breach, which would normally be equivalent to their wages for the period it would have taken to operate the procedure; and

- because contracts can only be varied with the agreement of both parties, any changes could only be made with the consent of the workforce or, where there is good reason for making the change, by giving the employees the same notice of the change as they would be entitled to receive to terminate their employment.

These problems can be overcome to some extent by including in the contract the right of management to change the rules and/or procedures and the right to shorten or vary the procedure at their discretion, although this may not do much to heighten employees' faith in the company's fairness.

Constructive Dismissal

Another aspect of common law to be considered is that it automatically implies into employees' contracts such terms as:

- a duty on employers to maintain the employment relationship;
- a duty of good faith; and
- a duty to pay salary/wages.

This means that employers who break any of these terms by, for instance, showing that they no longer have confidence in the employee (without good reason) or suspending an employee without pay (when there is no contractual provision allowing this course of action) will be in breach of contract and so the employee could resign and claim constructive dismissal.

The Need for Discipline

It may seem that it is better not to worry too much about maintaining a reasonable degree of order at work, and there are a variety of reasons often put forward for this: it would upset the unions; it would spoil the friendly atmosphere; the foreman or supervisor has recently been promoted and has to come to terms with no longer being "one of the lads"; it only gets you into legal problems; people work better if they are left alone, and so on.

These arguments can seem quite powerful, and it is worth examining them more fully, but the overriding point to remember is that the word "discipline" does not mean supervisors and managers must act like sergeant-majors. What we are talking about is, in the words of the ACAS Code of Practice on Discipline (see page 7):

> "Disciplinary rules and procedures are necessary for promoting fairness and order in the treatment of individuals and in the conduct of industrial relations. They also assist an organisation to operate effectively. Rules set standards of conduct at work; procedure helps to ensure that the standards are adhered to and also provides a fair method of dealing with alleged failures to observe them."

It is this definition that forms the keynote of this book: it is the job of supervisors and managers at all levels to ensure that the part of the organisation that is within their control operates effectively, and that their behaviour towards employees who don't observe standards is fair.

A point to bear in mind is that when we are talking about disciplinary action, we are talking about two separate things:

- informal action — somebody comes in late, or does sloppy work, and you pull them up about it on the spot or, at a more serious level, you call them into your office and give them a good dressing down; and

15

- formal action — this will normally follow on from informal action or will be the first step in serious misconduct cases and this really means that the employee could be on the road to dismissal.

The rest of this chapter concentrates on looking at the reasons why all companies need rules and procedures that are known and understood by everyone.

Upsetting the Unions

When companies recognise trade unions, an important part of the shop steward's job is to represent his members when disciplinary action is being taken against them, and there is obviously scope for conflict with the union in this area. This, though, should be no reason for backing away from taking disciplinary action. There is nothing more likely to cause trouble than allowing people to get away with things over a period then, when an employee finally goes too far, coming the heavy hand.

It is unreasonable in most companies to expect that shop stewards will want to become involved with any activities that seem to range them on the side of management in disciplinary procedures, but if they are brought into the procedure automatically, as representatives of union members, and the procedure adopted is fair and is applied consistently, there is no need in the vast majority of cases for disciplinary action to turn into conflict.

Similarly, unions have a useful role to play in helping to formulate and review procedures; such an involvement will lend credence to the fact that the procedure exists to ensure that suspected breaches of discipline are handled fairly. To summarise then, the following situation will suit most companies:

- formulation of rules should be a management responsibility, but unions can usefully be consulted;
- formulation of procedures lends itself to joint agreement;
- initiating and carrying through disciplinary action should be a management responsibility, with shop stewards sticking to their role of representing their members' interests;
- periodic reviews of the procedure could well be undertaken jointly.

If disciplinary action of any sort has to be taken against a shop steward, then obviously a very careful approach has to be adopted to avoid the action being seen as an attack on the union itself, which can obviously lead to serious industrial relations problems. No formal action should be taken until the circumstances have been discussed with either a full-time union official or a more senior union representative.

Spoiling a Friendly Atmosphere

It is often the case that supervisors and managers who take the line that to introduce formal disciplinary procedures would spoil the atmosphere, lead to reduced productivity, etc., are already applying such good standards that the lack of formal procedures has never been a problem, since difficulties have always been resolved in the informal stages. This, though, begs the question of what you do when faced with an employee who is totally intractable: who won't come into work on time, or who won't stop disrupting other people.

This sort of behaviour will usually have one of two results: either the other employees will see that employee getting away with murder and so will relax their own standards, or they will become very angry with the supervisor/manager for allowing the person to "get away with it". Neither of these situations makes for a friendly atmosphere and, of course, a good supervisor or manager will not let the situation drift too far. What, though, should be done? No matter how fair the procedure you adopt might seem to you, if it comes as a complete break from normal practice — and so from the employee's expectations — trouble will result.

Another difficulty is that action may well be taken in the heat of the moment, and such action is more likely than not to depart from the rules of fairness and natural justice. The same considerations apply when the philosophy is that people are better left on their own. They are, so long as you can rely on them, but you could still meet with one intractable employee.

One of the Lads

One of the most difficult situations to cope with is promotion to supervisor or manager of your own department. Overnight, you have to change from being a workmate to being responsible for order and output.

This transition can be made much easier if your company has well defined rules and procedures: without opting out of your new responsibilities, you can point out to the people you are supervising that both you and they know the rules, they know the procedure for enforcing them and they must appreciate that you have got to stick to them otherwise the people above you in the organisation could start using that same procedure on you for falling down on the job! Without any guidelines to begin with your life will be much more difficult.

The Legal Problems

It may be tempting to decide that to avoid getting involved with the law you will back out of the whole discipline scene, either by doing nothing more than giving a good 'rollicking', or by passing on the problems to your boss. In some cases, your own company's policy might be that no formal steps can be taken by you without having further authority: that's fine, but if discipline is your responsibility then you are going to run into a lot of problems. Once your own subordinates realise that you're not prepared to take any action yourself they could well make your life a misery, and you won't exactly endear yourself to your own boss by constantly insisting that he does your dirty work.

Nobody is suggesting that, just because there are now laws on unfair dismissal, you must think or act like a solicitor. Remember that the law only expects companies to act in a fair and reasonable way. It demands no more, on the whole, than is necessary for the sake of maintaining good relations between management and workforce.

Developing Employees

The most positive aspect of discipline is "development". Indisciplined employees will not give the best of themselves and their performance will be below that of which they are capable. Their indiscipline is met with complaint and reprimand by those in authority over them, and often enough their fellow workers as well who see them as abusing the situation or creating waves for everyone else by forcing the manager to take notice and tighten things up. The working relationship between those in authority and the employees they are responsible for is one of swings and roundabouts with most of the participants opting for a quiet life when the crunch comes. More often than not inertia is the response to potential conduct problems that could be recognised at quite an early stage, but remain untackled by supervisors and managers; possibly because the procedures are not there or, if they are there, they are just not used until the "last straw" situation arrives. All chances of salvaging the employees and making them valued contributors to the organisation have gone. Those young and inexperienced recruits whose knowledge of work is limited, members of the "awkward squad", the sly, rule stretchers and the "you owe me a living" types soon find that there is an irresistible force propelling them "down the road" with their cards in hand.

Not many tears will be shed for the worst of them but there are often fellow travellers who would, but for the lack of timely action by their supervisor or manager, still be doing a useful job.

Initiating such remedial action must be seen as a major responsibility for anyone who is in charge of staff, be they section leader, entrepreneur or manager, because even in a recession no one can afford to be profligate with talent (not to mention the recruitment and training costs involved). The best controllers of staff know that in the majority of cases the right word at the right time to an apparently erring employee is all that is required and counselling will often be a more satisfactory method of dealing with matters than formal disciplinary procedures. If in the end the formal procedures have to be used, the unpleasant legal consequences of unfair dismissal can usually be avoided; supervisors and managers have been seen to have acted fairly in giving the employee "a good length of rope" before dismissing him and the employee himself will leave that employment feeling "well they did give me every chance — it was a fair cop".

The Financial Costs

Finally, it has to be said that the financial costs incurred by the company when supervisors and managers neglect their 'discipline' role can be enormous, whether the costs have to be counted in terms of lost production — due to absenteeism, lateness, lack of skill or downright idleness — and, in the case of dismissals which could have been avoided if appropriate remedial action had been taken at the right time, in the cost of advertising for, recruiting and training new employees.

Conclusion

Simply the fact that you have, and work by, rules and procedures for dealing with misconduct won't, by itself, smooth out the difficulties you will inevitably have to face at some time. Hopefully, though, you will now accept that there is a need to use the procedures, and the remainder of this book is aimed at giving practical advice and tips to help you deal with the wide variety of the problems that fall under the "discipline" umbrella.

The Role of the First Line Manager

It is not within the scope of this chapter to enter into a detailed discussion of the role of the first line manager. It is a very complex job and we will only be concentrating on the manager's practical and effective approach to maintaining standards within his department. Firstly, let us pose the problem: who is the first line manager?

Everyone working with staff who can decide the priority, quality and quantity of work that those staff undertake must consider themselves as having first line responsibility for discipline. That affects all levels of management including managing directors (for their secretary, personal assistant, etc.), branch managers (for their administrative staff, departmental managers, etc.), section leaders in a factory, and even the senior typist who is in charge of the office junior. Sooner or later an issue arises in the best run departments which requires putting an end to unacceptable behaviour or emphasising the proper standards of job performance.

The fact that someone has to take responsibility to discipline is very much the crux of the problem. "Alice never gets things right and is a terrible timekeeper, perhaps Mr. So and So in the Personnel Department will have a word with her!" This is shifting the responsibility from where it quite correctly lies and in the process can actually damage the relationship between the supervisor and the employee. Too frequently employees are heard to say "Why couldn't he have told me that my work wasn't alright? Why did he have to involve someone else?"

To be really effective, the first informal step should always be taken by the employee's immediate supervisor who hopefully knows the employee quite well and will be the person who is immediately aware of any improvements as a result of their talk.

Most organisations delegate the authority to give informal reprimands to the employee's immediate supervisor so that minor everyday problems of conduct and job performance can be dealt with swiftly.

Most supervisors would say that they don't have the time to involve themselves in the welfare problems of those they supervise and would not wish to see that aspect of their job assume greater significance, especially if there is a personnel department with welfare responsibilities. Many supervisors and managers would say that it just wasn't their business to enquire into the personal life of those they supervise. Indeed they would argue that just the problems of maintaining production, whether it be on the factory floor, the typing pool or in the executive suite, is all they have time to do. However, supervisors of staff who do take this approach cannot expect to be as effective as those who do take responsibility because their decisions do not take into account relevant information and are often wildly inappropriate. You need only look at the welter of tribunal cases to see how some of their decisions have come expensively to grief.

It is not necessary to go overboard; it is simply a question of asking if there are any personal problems preying on the employee's mind that may be affecting his attitude to work. The individual personal circumstances do have a large bearing on job performance. (Particularly look out for the previously adequate employee who dramatically falls off in performance.) Very often solutions occur as a result of these enquiries, i.e. a week's compassionate leave, a change of department or job, the short term change of starting time to allow aged parents to be supervised until a more permanent arrangement can be made, etc. Such action can sort out the problem effectively whilst formal disciplinary warnings alone would have exacerbated the situation by increasing the pressure on an already pressurised employee.

Welfare Concern does not Prevent Disciplinary Action

Knowing the personal circumstances that the employee finds himself in does not prevent disciplinary action being taken in the end: employers are not required to go on sympathising indefinitely with the employee with personal problems that spill over into his job performance. There comes a time when the employer must demand that standards are kept regardless of these personal problems so that his business or the smooth operation of his department does not suffer. Consequently, it is important for the employee to know where and when the line will be drawn and this can be done more formally if the informal approach does not work.

Finding all Relevant Facts

Finding out if there are personal problems in mitigation is only one aspect of the supervisor's vital role in gathering the facts of the case together before deciding what to do. The most important part of the exercise is getting "genned up"' about the complaint you are going to make to the employee so that you can combat worthless excuses and state the complaint with some precision. For instance, is the work performance really worse than the rest of the department (what data supports such a contention); what does the analysis of the attendance records show; is the bulk of the lost time a result of a stay in hospital which has now corrected the problem or is it unexplained absence which amazingly always falls on a Monday or a Friday? In other words, make sure of your facts before tackling the employee concerned and make a note of the points that should be covered with him so that no relevant aspect is missed.

Consistency

As if to prove that working "through" people isn't easy there is another problem inherent in the role of the supervisor: consistency. It is only human to have preferences; to tolerate a little more from one employee whilst coming down like a ton of bricks on another, but to do it blatantly is always a dangerous practice and does nothing to build up trust in the supervisor's fairmindedness. It simply does not pay to have favourites so far as discipline is concerned. Consistency also means consistency over a period of time. With some supervisors, control is lacking and slack timekeeping becomes custom and practice in their department. Other "nodded-at" practices develop through sheer lethargy, e.g. unworked overtime may be allowed, arrangements to slow the machine's output to create overtime, etc. may be condoned over a long period of time.

Now, to tighten up and change these working practices it is necessary to give ample warning and explanation as to why it is no longer an acceptable practice. The new requirement, i.e. where the line is now drawn, should be stated precisely so that no one is in doubt and a clear indication is given that disciplinary action will be taken if that line is disregarded. Just to start dishing out warnings and reprimands without making it clear that "it's a new ball game" would be quite inappropriate and of course employers who recognise a trade union will in many cases have to consult with the union and perhaps buy out the practice before taking action. So, major changes in working practices in a department ought to be properly discussed with other managers who may at a later stage find themselves being involved.

There is a great deal to be said for supervisors and managers trying to establish an agreed approach for dealing with minor misconduct, poor performance, etc., within an organisation. Even talking over a problem with others similarly placed in charge of employees, rather than struggling alone, can provide an important chance to pool experience and agree standards which are consistent throughout the organisation.

To summarise, the person with first line supervisory responsibilities for discipline has four key areas in which to operate:

● establishing and maintaining standards of acceptable conduct and work performance of the employees over whom direct control is exercised;

● consistently upholding these standards, as far as humanly possible, without fear or favour (unless there is a good reason for adopting another view of the matter or taking different action);

● halting unacceptable behaviour at the outset with an appropriate word at the right time, i.e. too much talking, untidy work, general messing about, bad language, etc., and dealing with aspects of conduct and performance that deteriorate over a period of time;

● the proper investigation and formulation of the complaint concerning poor conduct or job performance prior to informally taking the employee to task about it.

Giving informal warnings or counselling can be a difficult situation for anyone, even a supervisor with many years of experience behind him, and the following section of the book deals with some of the pitfalls and strategies that might help when tackling an employee "face to face".

Informal Action is Important

The informal warning or reprimand is probably the most important step in the whole disciplinary process because this is where the best chances exist to get the employee to conform and perform correctly. It is also a step that is easy to convince yourself to avoid because of the fear of mishandling.

There really are no standard formulae for handling people; sensitivity, applied commonsense and knowing what must be achieved by the confrontation is all that supervisors and managers have to rely on. Flexibility of approach is essential so that account can be taken of the situations and personalities involved. There are, however, lots of useful wrinkles and drills which can be picked up from the day to day experience of controlling staff. This isn't much comfort for the newly promoted supervisor or manager who is faced with his first discipline problem after years of successful management, and a few guidelines should help just to get started.

Additionally, the arrival of vast quantities of employment legislation, and the involvement of unions, result in many employers and their responsible staff saying that they are frightened to take any action to pull up employees who are behaving badly — as one wag said, he was frightened to give anyone a rollicking in case he inadvertently constructively dismissed them!!

Clearly, if there is a reluctance to get involved in "face to face" disciplinary situations it is because supervisors and managers want to know "what can I say?" "what do I do when they react?", "if all goes horribly wrong how can I recover my position without complete loss of face?" "how far can I go?" and "what is my legal position?" It is the answers to these and many more questions we hope to provide.

The first step is deciding whether any approach should be made to the employee — is it a trivial matter and if not, how serious is it and has it occurred before?

Check List: Should Action be Taken?

1. Is the matter trivial and worth overlooking or must informal or formal disciplinary action be taken early on to prevent recurrence?

   Things to Bear In Mind

   (a) Will the conduct be potentially dangerous or lead to financial loss?

   (b) Is it conduct that shows a deeper disrespect for those in authority?

   (c) Is it conduct that encourages others to copy and therefore get out of control?

   (d) Are the errors in performance fundamental to the successful performance of the employee's job?

   (e) Is it conduct in breach of a rule or regulation that is not normally enforced?

   (f) Is it conduct that annoys, irritates or offends other workers?

   If the answer to any of these questions is yes, then action must be taken to correct.

2. Has any informal or formal action been taken before? If it has, this will determine at what level you start taking disciplinary action. Check personnel records and any personal record kept of informal disciplinary action.

3. Formulate precisely what the complaint is, check the facts and get the evidence together. (This won't take very long in most circumstances but, in some cases, may involve taking statements from employees who saw the incidents and other detailed investigation. Where this is going to be a lengthy process the employee concerned should be suspended on full pay.)

4. If necessary check company disciplinary procedure and consult with the personnel department and immediate superior before deciding whether informal action is necessary or, because of the serious nature of the matter, a direct entry into formal disciplinary action is desirable.

On-the-Job Reprimand

If it is a clear cut situation involving minor misconduct such as inattention to work, too much talking, untidy work, etc., then often a verbal reprimand can be given immediately. This is quite distinct from a chivying remark or giving supplementary instructions: it indicates that the limits of acceptable behaviour have been reached.

It is important that the reprimand is done carefully. The purpose is not to humiliate the individual in front of his fellow workers as this encourages an aggressive response which may be difficult to handle, others may be tempted to get involved in the matter and in an instant the matter can get out of control. Try to settle the matter in private. Always avoid abusiveness and do not personalise the reprimand (references to prominent racial characteristics, smallness of stature or doubts about his parentage are best not said). Withering sarcasm is also very destructive especially to younger employees. Most employees, if approached in this manner, "turn off" — they cease to listen to anything that is said to them — they don't participate in the disciplinary process and the chance of successfully obtaining their co-operation and respect is reduced.

It goes without saying that at all times getting involved in arguments is taboo. If one starts to develop, just listen. Then reassert your position when the employee has run out of steam. Physical contact should also be avoided — even a guiding outstretched arm can be misinterpreted. Such interviews are usually unplanned and often carried out in less than ideal circumstances, surrounded by noisy machinery, a constant flow of customers, and lacking privacy. Somehow the supervisor has to find the time to deal immediately with the problem and find a suitable place to converse with the employee concerned.

To assist in these objectives, a useful drill to follow is outlined below:

● if you have lost your cool, indicate that you will deal with the matter shortly and go and calm down;

● call the employee away from his workplace, preferably to an office or to a place out of earshot and view of others — seating will not always be available. If more than one employee is involved explain that you wish to see them one at a time. Emphasise that the same thing will be said to each person involved. Avoid being put under pressure by being outnumbered;

● some supervisors find preliminary calming down tactics like offering a cigarette or a cup of tea a useful way of "heading off" an aggressive reaction or reassuring the employee that the interview will only be as unpleasant as necessary to make the point adequately. It certainly is a good idea to find time to compose yourself and allow the employees' mood to decline and their wariness to subside. Sending out for the union representative is often a way to do this if your company's disciplinary procedure requires the attendance of the representative at any disciplinary interview. Don't forget to ask if they want a friend (employed by the company) present whilst you are talking to them. Most will decline;

- explain in measured tones what they have done and why it is not acceptable or sensible. Ask if there is any explanation they wish to offer (the chap who is in deep water for tossing a piece of wood at another employee may have been plagued by spitballs propelled by his mates for most of the morning — you ought to deal with the provocateur as well);

- try always to observe the normal social courtesies. Try to avoid raising your voice, limit your body movements when speaking (don't fiddle with paperclips or cigarette boxes) and don't go into a great diatribe, so be as brief and as clear as possible. Vague, embarrassed waffle is as exasperating and ineffective as too blunt an approach which alienates;

- try and avoid tension in body posture, facial expression and your voice. Keep eye contact with the employee, not to stare him out but to emphasise the things you are saying in a relaxed way. Your face should register seriousness of purpose because verbal reprimands given whilst smiling or joking are not effective;

- summarise the situation at the end of the interview. Make sure the employee is told that the conversation must be treated as an informal verbal warning/reprimand;

- make a note of the incident in a diary or general daybook, personnel record, etc;

- send the employee firmly back to work after asking him what his next tasks are.

Other situations can be more complicated and should ideally be given a more lengthy treatment even though the matter is being dealt with on the informal level. Thoroughness does pay off big dividends.

Firstly, we shall look at organising disciplinary interviews which in principle remain much the same at both the formal and informal levels, including how to cope if things start to go wrong and some strategies to adopt depending on the type of disciplinary problem that is being dealt with.

Organising Disciplinary Interviews

Problems such as lateness, absence, poor performance and attitude spread out over time and when dealing with these issues, more often than not it is the supervisor who picks the time and place to tackle the employee. This first approach should be done at an informal level in the first instance. Because the supervisor or manager is initiating the action there is little excuse for poor preparation and investigation which form the vital preliminary steps before a disciplinary interview.

Timing

Setting the time of that interview can sometimes be important. If weepy scenes or other difficulties are anticipated, set the time for late afternoon so that the employee can leave the premises as normal and not involve everyone else on the premises. Similarly, Fridays ought to be the popular day for disciplinary interviews so that employees have the weekend to think over the implications of the discussion. This is, of course, a difficult day for most people because wages are paid and time may be difficult to find. You may also have to arrange for the recognised trade union steward to be present if it is a requirement of the company disciplinary procedure. Remember that if a dispute arises over the facts of the incident you may have to call in witnesses to support your allegations. (This is more likely to happen in serious misconduct matters which are dealt with at the formal levels of procedure.)

Surroundings

Don't ignore the physical setting of the interview. Beg, borrow or steal an office or place where you will not be disturbed — somewhere quiet, with available seating. Leave instructions to prevent phone calls being put through to you. The employee must be aware that a special effort is being directed towards him to grab his attention. With employees who are on first name terms and social companions of those in charge of them, it is difficult for the supervisor to "distance" himself, to adopt a concerned but detached attitude when disciplining employees and there is a temptation to do nothing until a last straw. This means that the employer or supervisor loses his temper and a good old fashioned rollicking results. Dismissals that occur like this are usually unfair, with all the financial liability that that involves.

"Distancing"

The important point is to show the employee that you are putting on your "authority hat" — "distancing" yourself. This can be done by using a more formal way of speaking. "Peter I must ask you to come to my office, I would like to have a serious talk with you". If you maintain eye contact as well Peter will be in no doubt that you are being serious and will twig that you are going to take him to task about something.

It is the particular problem of all small or family companies that the swings and roundabouts style of management prevails. So how do you deal with it?

Surprisingly, such pull-ups often come as a relief to an employee who realises he has been living dangerously. In summary, don't wait until the relationship is irreparably fractured; deal with the problem before it reaches the hair-tearing out stage and dismissal is the only possible outcome. It is only human nature to see how far you can go before someone blows the whistle, so don't think that relationships must become permanently damaged.

Useful Hints on Face to Face Meetings

Having ushered the employee into an office (some thought should have been given to the setting so that the seating arrangement has been sorted out beforehand) invite the employee to sit down. The serious intent of the conversation will be reinforced by the supervisor taking a seat behind a table or desk. Don't use psychological ploys like making the employee face into the light whilst you remain in the shadow or keep him standing whilst you are seated, there is no need to use MI5 tactics and at this informal level there is no need for any witnesses. Make sure that you can hear each other easily, so don't sit too far apart; make sure you are not constantly interrupted with people coming in, and if this happens apologise to the employee for the intrusion. Preliminary tactics discussed on page 27 help to compose both the supervisor and the employee and help to set the scene for constructive conversations. Observe all the normal courtesies: raving about the office or hammering on the desk with your fist is almost always counterproductive. The whole purpose of the interview is to tell the employee, in measured tones, without losing your temper or raising your voice, the reason for your dissatisfaction. If the employee starts to vociferously defend himself (after all attack is the best form of defence) — listen. You don't lose face by listening but you do if you start to browbeat and shout him down.

If you have made some brief notes (yes it's a good idea) on all the points you wish to talk to him about, insist that you wish to go through them point by point and then hear what he has to say to each one. Make it clear that you are not dissatisfied with everything, some aspects of his job performance may be very good whilst his timekeeping may be appalling. You should take the opportunity to give pats on the back as well as brickbats. This will confirm to the employee that the discussion will be a constructive situation in which encouragement will be given — good behaviour will be rewarded. The employee will be more inclined to co-operate and won't mentally "shut-off" and stop listening.

Documents

If there are any data or documents, i.e. production output figures, attendance, timekeeping records, letter of complaint from a customer, etc., then show them to the employee and explain your interpretation of them. Give the employee an indication of what you think is going wrong and why he is falling below standard. Here, you must seize the opportunity to get the employee to offer his explanations or reasons as to why he is failing to reach the expected standard. Encourage the search for these reasons by suggesting some yourself.

Interview Should not be One-Sided

Get the employee to speak — a disciplinary interview is a two-way process not just a one-sided harangue. See if there are any personal problems that are having an unsettling effect and may account for him falling below standard. If the employee won't discuss these problems with you, offer the chance to speak to the personnel officer or another manager. If there is still a reluctance, then you can only explain that if personal problems are relevant you won't be able to take them into account when assessing the situation.

Assessing the Employee's Excuses

You will have to consider what validity any of the reasons given have, because they may be sufficient for you to reconsider your actions in giving an informal warning. This is another function of the disciplinary interview, to ensure that all relevant information is assessed before the warning is given. If there is any doubt about the appropriateness of the warning — don't give it. The disciplinary interview does help to avoid embarrassing mistakes. Sometimes a totally different set of facts are brought to light by the employee. You will have to check them out if there is any likelihood that they are true, e.g. an employee may have been given a different set of instructions by another manager which he has acted upon, or the down time on their machine has affected output and this was beyond their control (you may find it necessary to suspend the interview and resume later after these revelations have been checked).

You must consider: do the reasons actually account for the poor performance? Were the matters complained of within the employee's control or the fault of the organisation, or someone else? Do not be afraid to tell the employee that their reasons are substantial and that you will be taking no further action except to try and iron out the problem at source. This is another main objective of the disciplinary meeting, to eliminate the problem, not just to chastise the employee.

If on the other hand you find that the reasons given are merely an excuse, then you should plainly say so. Do not give the impression that you have accepted an excuse when you think it is irrelevant or implausible. Don't be angry at prevarication, it is perfectly natural to try to excuse yourself when confronted.

Searching for Solutions

The next step in the interview is to reinforce to the employees, whatever the excuses, that the situation is unacceptable and ask them what are they going to do about improving their conduct or performance? Of course, you will also consider if there are any steps the company can take to help the situation, i.e. temporary changes to the hours of work, retraining, etc.

Search for the solution together and try to get the employee's commitment to a remedial course of action because in the long term his continued employment will depend on its success.

Before sending the employee back to work draw the interview to a close and summarise what has been talked about under the following headings:

- the complaint and the reasons why this is not an acceptable standard of behaviour/performance;
- the reasons given by the employee for this failure and any arrangements or remedial action agreed, including any time period over which matters will be reviewed;
- what the next steps are if there is no improvement (refer to the company's formal disciplinary procedures, if there are any).

It may be necessary to discuss any special arrangements with senior managers first, and if the go-ahead is given send some written confirmation to the employee (especially if it involves a temporary change of contractual terms like hours of work or special leave of absence). Make sure all the conditions attached to such an arrangement are specified, i.e. length of time, with or without pay, etc., in the letter.

Things May Go Wrong

It would be too much to expect that every disciplinary interview will go smoothly. Though, surprisingly, most will be "doddles" if the problems have been caught at an early stage. Some particular problems encountered are given below.

Women

Women can present a problem to a male supervisor or manager because they might cry when they are told off. (It is interesting that most female supervisors don't have this problem or perhaps they are undeterred by it or the women employees realise it.) They may be entirely genuine tears but they shouldn't prevent the interview from being completed. Offer to get a drink of water, perhaps a couple of aspirins, hand over a paper handkerchief and tell her to "dry your eyes and we'll continue when you have composed yourself (however long it takes)".

When the employee realises that the situation cannot be avoided she is usually prepared to continue. If the waterworks break out again use the same tactic or, perhaps, if the employee is considerably agitated suspend the interview until the following day. Whatever happens, once started, the interview must be completed. Threats to "bring their husbands round" shouldn't be taken lightly. You should respond with full magisterial authority: point out that she is the one who is employed, that she is more than capable of putting her own case, and you will listen to what she has to say. If she is making threats of violent behaviour by her husband then she is putting herself seriously in the wrong to the point, in fact, where her dismissal may be the outcome. Continue the interview and just hope you are bigger than he is or that he's a reasonable man. Incidentally, before starting to interview a woman employee it may be sensible to leave the door open or ensure than someone can observe the meeting without actually being involved with it. Sometimes, highly colourful allegations can be made and no male supervisor should put himself into the position that he can't prove otherwise.

Involvement of Union Representatives

In companies where the recognised shop steward is involved at the informal stages, the degree to which he participates depends on custom and practice. Ideally, one should aim to confine him to the role of observer and allow him to give advice to his member outside the door or in another office. If the steward is going to be present and is likely to be articulate on the employee's behalf make sure another member of the management team is present to observe the proceedings and provide advice.

Gross Misconduct During the Interview

Sometimes the response to being carpeted can be explosive: cups of coffee can be poured over the interviewing supervisor, fists can start to fly or the language deteriorates to the extent that it is intolerable. If physical violence is offered then, providing it was unprovoked by the interviewer, it should be dealt with as a gross misconduct situation. Firstly, restrain the employee, call for help if necessary, then suspend him and send him off the company premises with instructions to return the next day for the matter to be considered. Then arrange for a senior manager to review the situation next day at an interview with the employee and decide whether or not to dismiss. Many company rules provide for insubordinate behaviour and bad language to be treated as acts of gross misconduct, and the same sort of procedure should be adopted as that stated below. Even if the supervisor does have the authority to dismiss, as he cannot be considered a disinterested party, it is better to have someone uninvolved to adjudicate on the matter after a period of suspension. Usually, when the employee returns, he is ready to apologise and the interview can be completed. It is always sensible to allow the employee to climb down gracefully when he has done things in the heat of the moment and a final warning would be appropriate punishment, though much depends on what he actually did when he was angry.

Storming Out

Getting the employee into the interview is easy but having him stay and co-operate to the end is much harder. Once again employees use avoidance tactics. You should make it clear to the employee that if he leaves the office it is in defiance of your reasonable instructions, that you will take it further, to a senior manager, and dismissal may result. If that doesn't work, say that you are suspending the interview until the next working day when he's calmed down and then you will continue where you left off. If he doesn't think he should be carpeted then tell him of the right of appeal (according to the company's appeal procedure) to a senior manager. The reconvened interview had then better take place with the senior manager present.

Don't lose heart, because these situations are rare and are usually the result of a volatile employee being tackled too late. It must be clear to anyone that an employee acting so unreasonably is putting himself into an even worse position from which he can't win.

Solicitors and Other Ploys

The ways of dealing with the problems given above are not the only solutions neither are they the only disrupting situations that can happen. Many managers are thoroughly discomfitted when employees demand the presence of their solicitors or a copy of their contract of employment (a statement must be received within 13 weeks of starting employment and very often it is overlooked), or younger workers may demand that their mum or dad attends. Such positions are taken so that disciplinary action appears to be enormously difficult and full of unseen problems and the supervisor backs down as a result.

Actually, the answers are quite simple. In general, there is no right for employees to call their solicitors to be in attendance at disciplinary meetings and one is on fairly safe ground to refuse such a request. Similarly, mums and dads have no specific right to attend unless they are parties to an apprenticeship contract. (There are, of course, situations when it is a good idea to involve parents, especially when formal disciplinary procedures are being used.) Contracts of employment rarely have any bearing on the disciplinary requirements, minimum production requirements, etc., but this doesn't mean that a supervisor cannot quite validly take someone to task for failing to reach a reasonable standard.

Monitoring the Success of Informal Disciplinary Action

If a period of assessment or retraining, etc., has been arranged then allow this period to expire before deciding whether the required standards have been reached or if formal disciplinary action will now be necessary.

It is always sensible to make some effort to give special attention to an employee during this review period, both to encourage and to give guidance. Try and give them the feeling that you wish them to succeed in reaching the standards required and you aren't going to treat them like social pariahs because you are unhappy with some aspect of their job performance or embarrassed at having to take them to task over it.

If the necessary improvement has not been made then it is time for a formal disciplinary interview. Check your company procedures to see who has the authority to give this warning; it is usually a departmental manager or general manager. You will need to ensure that he takes action.

Note the dates when review periods come to an end in your diary and ensure that you reappraise the situation honestly when the time arrives. If the employee has made satisfactory improvement then tell him. If it is only qualified improvement and you would like to give him a little longer, once again, tell him and explain why there are still problem areas in job performance or conduct.

36

Checklist: Informal Disciplinary Interview

Preliminary Steps
1. Have you got the facts at your fingertips?
2. Have you obtained all the relevant written data and documents?
3. Have you defined precisely what your complaint is?
4. Have you thought of the excuses that might be offered and would they form a reasonable defence against your complaint? Investigate.
5. Have you made brief notes of the matters you intend to raise to prompt your memory and make sure you don't leave anything out?

Physical Organisation of the Interview
1. Is there a quiet place, out of earshot of others, where the employee can be spoken to in private?
2. Is there adequate seating?
3. Have instructions been left that no one should disturb the meeting whether by phone or physical intrusion?
4. Does the company disciplinary procedure require the recognised trade union representative to be present? If that is the case, ensure he knows about the meeting.
5. Have cigarettes or coffee organised to help put the employee at ease.
6. Will anyone else be required to attend; if contended facts emerge will witnesses be needed?
7. Decide the best time to convene the interview.

Dos and Don'ts
1. Do not get involved in arguments.
2. Avoid physical contact.
3. Don't use the opportunity to harangue the employee: state the complaint as briefly and concisely as possible.
4. Don't raise your voice or become abusive, and observe the normal social courtesies.
5. Do not try to humiliate or make personal remarks.
6. Avoid sarcasm, particularly with younger employees.
7. Restrict your body movement whilst speaking and don't fiddle around with objects on the desk.

8. Try to avoid tension in the body posture, facial expression and in your voice.

9. Maintain eye contact with the employee.

10. Don't joke or smile extravagantly. Seriousness of purpose should be registered throughout.

Procedure

1. Tell the employee what the substance of the complaint is.

2. Show the employee any data to emphasise the point and explain it to him.

3. Ask the employee if there is any reason or mitigating circumstance that ought to be considered: encourage the employee to talk.

4. Consider the reasons/explanation put forward by the employee. Evaluate:
   (a) Is the employee entirely at fault or was someone else responsible? Was it an organisational failure?
   (b) If it was the employee's fault, are there any personal or other mitigating circumstances to take into account?
   (c) Are the explanations just excuses?

5. Ask the employee what he intends to do to remedy the situation?

6. Search jointly for a solution that will address the problem and allow the employee to make the necessary improvements.

7. Summarise the interview and make sure the employee is told that the interview must be treated as an informal warning and what steps will be taken next if improvements in performance or conduct are not forthcoming. Specify any time limits agreed for performance or conduct to be reviewed.

8. Make a note of the proceedings in a diary or on a file.

Monitoring

If time limits are agreed, ensure that you reinterview when that time limit has been reached. If satisfactory progress has been made, give a pat on the back. If progress is unsatisfactory you must take formal action as specified by the company disciplinary procedure. See Chapter on "Formal Procedure".

Formal Procedures

If all the efforts of the supervisor have failed at the informal stages without the necessary improvement being made then it's time to initiate a first level formal written warning and go through the procedure until it is finally exhausted. Sometimes more serious forms of misconduct may justify an immediate written warning. Outlined below is a checklist of considerations to be taken into account before taking steps to give a formal written warning.

Checklist: When to take Formal Disciplinary Action

1. Has any period of time for improvement been fully completed without the employee achieving the required standards with regard to their conduct or job performance?
2. Has the same or similar incident of minor misconduct, i.e. rudeness, inattention to work, etc., occurred again?
3. Has the incident occurred within a reasonable period of time after the informal warning? (Anything longer than 6 months would not be reasonable.)
4. Is the act of misconduct rather more serious than that which normally merits an informal warning?
5. Is the act of misconduct a breach of the written company rules for which a formal written warning is prescribed?

If the answer to any one of these questions is yes, then a formal warning should be given.

Where to Find the Procedures

Many organisations have written disciplinary procedures that have been agreed with the recognised trade union (if appropriate) and are incorporated into each individual employee's contract of employment by either being physically written into the terms and conditions statement or into an incorporated document like a company handbook, union agreement, etc. This has the distinct advantage that both parties know precisely what steps will be taken.

Why Keep to the Procedure

If there is a procedure laid down then you must follow it. Every supervisor or manager must thoroughly read and understand exactly how the disciplinary procedure works. Even slight failures to follow the laid down procedure can cause problems with trade union officials, who will sieze on any procedural irregularity to defend their members. Furthermore, if the matter ultimately goes to an industrial tribunal the decision may go against the employer because of the oversight. There may be circumstances where failing to slavishly follow the procedure can be justified:

(a) where the procedure actually allows stages to be jumped for specific offences or at management discretion;

(b) by circumstances where in the disciplinary interview the employee indicates that he is clearly set on going his own way and will not co-operate or will not accept that he has done anything wrong.

Many other organisations have no written procedures at all to guide managers and supervisors in coping with disciplinary problems and neither are there any written rules or regulations setting out the standards of conduct required, so it may be useful to look at an example procedure that is based on the ACAS Code of Practice but has been adapted to a small non-unionised company. A very different kind of procedure will be required for a company where, say, there are many branch offices or shops or where there is a recognised trade union that will be involved in the disciplinary process.

Whatever the type of procedure adopted there are certain universal features and points to look out for when operating them.

Example Disciplinary Procedure for Small Non-Unionised Company

Objective

The purpose of the company's disciplinary procedure is to ensure the safe and effective operation of the business and the fair treatment of individual employees.

Procedures

1. Informal Warnings
Minor breaches of company discipline, misconduct, failure to maintain job performance standards, poor timekeeping, etc.,

will result in a verbal warning given by your immediate superior. A note of this warning will be made in daybook/clockcard/personnel record card/etc.

It is unlikely that any other further action will be necessary as in most cases a verbal warning will quickly resolve most difficulties.

Where there is a more serious breach of company discipline or misconduct or an employee fails to improve and maintain that improvement in relation to conduct or job performance formal disciplinary action will be taken.

2. Formal Warnings

● A disciplinary interview conducted by .... will be held. The employee may be accompanied by another employee of the company if he wishes.

● The employee will be informed of the nature of the complaint and such evidence as may exist. The employee may present his explanation of the matter.

● If it is decided that disciplinary action should be taken the employee will be told of the decision and later given a letter in confirmation.

● The employee will be told, and the written confirmation will state:

  (a) details of the misconduct, poor performance or other matter that has occasioned the warning;

  (b) details of the necessary action to remedy the situation, outlining precisely what standard is expected and any period of review, extra training, etc., decided on;

  (c) that any further misconduct, or expiry of the review period without significant and sustained improvement, will result in:

    (i) dismissal with appropriate contractual notice, or

    (ii) a further disciplinary interview and confirmed final warning which, if unheeded, will result in dismissal with the appropriate notice.

● The final decision to dismiss can only be taken by .... after he has satisfied himself with regard to the facts of the case; whether or not there are any mitigating circumstances, and interviewing the employee concerned.

- Some alternatives short of dismissal may be considered. They are as follows:
  - (a) suspension without pay up to a maximum of 7 days;
  - (b) demotion and associated loss of pay to a more suitable job, if available;
  - (c) transfer to other premises, department, etc.

3. Dismissal Without Warnings

In rare circumstances the employee will be summarily dismissed without notice if it is established, after investigation and hearing the employee's version of the matter, that there has been an act of gross misconduct, major breach of duty or conduct that brings the company into disrepute. In particular this includes:

insubordination;

serious breach of safety rules potentially involving loss of life or limb;

theft or fraud;

breach of clocking rules;

being under the influence of drink or drugs during working hours;

flagrant failure to follow company documentary procedures or regulations;

breach of duty regarding non-disclosure of confidential information;

deliberate damage to company property or that of other employees;

disorderly or indecent conduct, fighting on company premises or threatening physical violence;

acts of incitement or actual acts of discrimination on the grounds of sex, race, religion, colour or ethnic origin.

4. Suspension

At any stage of the disciplinary procedure the employee may be suspended with pay whilst the circumstances of any complaint are being investigated.

5. Appeals

At any stage of the disciplinary procedure the employee may appeal to .... either verbally or in writing against any disciplinary action taken against him providing it is done within 48 hours of that action being taken.

Key Aspects of Operating the Procedure

1. Object of the Procedure

The employer who drafted the procedure outlined above is to be congratulated because he avoided calling the procedure a "dismissal" procedure! The objective is clearly stated in the opening paragraph and indicates the spirit and intention of the procedure — it is remedial; all employees have access to it (sometimes employers do have different procedures for different groups of workers) and its aim is to rehabilitate. Supervisors and managers have a clear responsibility to operate disciplinary procedures in this manner. It's not just a way to get rid of people whilst appearing to go through the motions of a fair dismissal.

Now, keeping to some of the highly developed (longwinded) procedures can be infuriating to a supervisor who knows he has a "bad one" and wants to get rid of him quickly. However, there is nothing more unpleasant than doing it in a hurry and then having a tribunal decision awarded against you, and the information filtering back to other employees in the company in a highly distorted way. "Softly, softly, catchee monkey" is the best approach.

2. Informal Warnings, Reprimands

The section on informal warnings makes no mention of an interview but this is by far the best way to operate the procedure at every stage. (A closer look at informal procedures is contained in the Chapter beginning on page 25.)

It is not just a pious hope that in most cases there will be no need to go further than this informal level. Most employees only require to be spoken to in a constructive, clear way and they will try to put matters right. If the employee does not, for whatever reason, there is a provision in the procedure to give formal written warnings. Most procedures allow for this informal stage to be left out in a more serious case of misconduct.

Many companies operate a totting-up system whereby lateness and absence warnings are totted-up and counted together, i.e. six informal warnings in three months for either reason results in a formal written warning. Special care must be taken when operating such a procedure because it soon becomes apparent that some employees have become experts at working the system, i.e. never getting the sixth informal warning and relying on the six months' life span of the warning to write off old offences (some written procedures only give a three month life span for informal warnings). Some appallingly bad attendance records are fuelled by such disciplinary procedures and require a little ingenuity on the part of the supervisor to make disciplinary action effective (see Chapter on Practical Application). Without such a totting-up system, great care should be exercised to ensure that it is only repeats of the same offence that are dealt with progressively by disciplinary action. An informal warning for lateness cannot be followed in the first instance with a written warning for absence and later, a final warning for poor workmanship.

3. How to Give a Written Warning
It is important to note that even at the formal stages great priority is given to holding a disciplinary interview. There should be no attempt at avoiding a "face to face" session with the employee by just jotting off a few lines of complaint and warning, popping it in the post box or leaving it in a sealed envelope on his desk or in a pay packet. Tribunals utterly deplore this kind of approach and quite rightly so. It is also an ineffective method of getting commitment from an employee to change his ways. Additionally, the employee has no chance to state his case, give details of any mitigating circumstances and correct any inaccuracies in the facts that have told against him. It is most embarrassing to be forced to withdraw warnings that cannot be substantiated and in some circumstances it could give grounds for the employee to claim constructive dismissal.

4. Company at the Interview
Even if the procedure does not state that the employee may be accompanied at the interview it is always a good idea to ask if they would like someone else to be present (see section on Formal Disciplinary Interview, page 55).

5. Prior Indication
In many circumstances the employee can be given some indication of the purpose of the meeting before he goes into it. This is good practice because he will have a chance to consider what is being alleged against him and sort out what he is going to say in his own defence. It may well be that he will choose to get some advice from his union, solicitor or citizens advice bureau.

(No union official may attend such a meeting without agreement of the parties unless the union is recognised.

Similarly, solicitors do not have a right to attend though very often employers agree to such a move when they know their case is strong so that justice can be seen to be done. In principle it is not a good idea to involve non-company personnel in such an interview.)

6. When The Letter Should Be Given

The main ground rules for disciplinary meetings have already been discussed on page 29 and will be dealt with again in the next section. The main difference now that we have entered the formal part of the procedure is that a formal written document results, a copy of which is given to the employee after the disciplinary interview. Don't be tempted to write it up complete with signature and hand it to the employee at the beginning or at the end of the interview. This would indicate a very cynical approach which would show that you were just going through the motions. Anything the employee might say on his own behalf wouldn't be listened to or considered.

There is no need for the employee to sign the written warning, particularly if a disciplinary interview takes place before it is issued, because it is simply an accurate confirmation of what was said.

So far as accepting warnings is concerned, the employee is in a difficult position: the only effective way of protesting a warning is to appeal to a company director or follow whatever procedure is specified to accomplish an appeal against disciplinary action. If that fails, then his only recourse is to leave his employment and claim constructive dismissal on the basis that the warning was completely contrived in order to get rid of him. Ripping up the warning will have no effect and the employer may consider it served if he formally reads the contents to the employee and consigns the copy to the individual's personnel file.

7. Procedural Flexibility

The example procedure given has a great deal of flexibility built into it, which is ideal for a small company. It is not realistic to expect a lengthy procedure going to three written warnings before a final written warning is reached from a small company where employees are well known and disharmony can be deeply destructive. They do not have the same resources as larger organisations and all employees must pull their weight. In larger companies an employee may have several supervisors during the course of a year and extensive written procedures are the only way to keep tabs on things. These several levels of formal written warnings are usually a response to the size of the organisation and the degree of unionisation.

All the law requires is that a fair procedure is used. Although the ACAS Code of Practice (see page 7) sets out guidelines, there are many ways a disciplinary procedure can be fashioned without following it in every detail, yet still remain a fair procedure. In the example at the beginning of this chapter the option is given to either have a final written warning or a first written warning depending on the nature of the misconduct and other mitigating circumstances, like previous long unblemished service, personal circumstances, etc., that may be taken into account.

8. Life Span of Warnings

In the example procedure there is no life span laid down for these warnings and there is a good reason for this. If a situation arose where a senior manager is found to have worked in competition with his company it would normally justify his immediate dismissal. If, however, he had important skills and was prepared to agree that he would not continue such a practice, he might well be given a final written warning specifying that if he was disloyal again he would be dismissed. It would be essential to give a formal warning to show that the conduct was not approved or condoned and it would be nonsense for such a warning only to have a six month life span.

Simply, it depends on the nature of the offence, the seniority of the employee and what is considered reasonable in the circumstances. In general, warnings for minor offences can only be valid for a maximum of 6 months whilst more serious offences that result in final warnings may remain in force for 12 months or more. Do not try to use old expired warnings to build a case against an employee or incidents for which no warning was given at the time.

9. Final Warning and Dismissal

Once again, if there has been no improvement or the same misconduct is committed again, the next stage in the procedure is initiated. If a first warning had been given, then another interview will confirm a final warning. If the last warning was a final one that threatened dismissal, then the interview will revolve around the possibility of finding some lesser penalty than dismissal (in most cases this will not be possible).

Any final decision to dismiss is usually reserved for a senior manager or director who, if he has not been involved up to now, must familiarise himself with the case and interview the employee. If a tribunal action results he most certainly will be required to give evidence and dismissal by remote control is not very convincing even if he was acting on reports of other managers.

Appeals

It is quite usual for disciplinary procedures to contain an appeals procedure so that if the employee is dissatisfied and doesn't believe he has received a fair hearing, he should be told or reminded of the existence of this procedure, and that it can be used at any stage when warnings are given. In effect, it is a safety valve to check that things have been done properly and to ensure that bias is eliminated.

This appeals provision is quite separate from the normal grievance procedure which employees use when they want to complain about always being put on a job they don't like, or having to work with a particular person, or when they feel that refusal of holiday leave or their grading is unfair.

Example Grievance Procedure for Small Non-Unionised Companies

If an employee wishes to discuss a grievance or raise a query arising from his or her employment, the matter should be raised with the immediate supervisor. If a satisfactory solution is not reached in 3 working days the employee can raise the matter with a director of the company. This can be done either verbally or in writing.

After consultation, the director will give his decision within 5 working days. There are no further levels of appeal. This procedure applies to both individual and collective grievances.

Disciplinary appeals procedures, on the other hand, usually only have one level and it is directed to the top of the management structure. Sometimes there is provision for the matter to go to arbitration. This enables the decision to be reviewed by someone with the authority to promptly put it right if it was a bad decision.

Even in small companies where the employer is effectively involved in all levels of discipline, including the decision to dismiss, an appeals procedure will allow a review at a more composed and less harassed time. Ideally, the employee should be interviewed by the person hearing the appeal. There is no reason for the decision to be given there and then; a letter explaining the reasons for the rejection (or acceptance) later would be quite permissible. The person hearing the appeal may well think it sensible to do his own checking if the employee has thrown up anything interesting.

Some General Points

1. A question often asked is how soon after a final warning can we dismiss? Well, if the matter revolves around a specific act of misconduct, i.e. insubordination to a supervisor or smoking in a non-smoking area, the employee can be dismissed the next time he repeats the offence. If it is the type of offence for which patterns emerge over time, i.e. lateness, poor attendance, etc., then it is safer to give a period of review and when that period expires decide whether or not the required standard is met. If not, then dismissal will result.

2. Another question frequently posed is "we told him that we would give him three months to improve, he'll never make it so can we let him go now?" This may be quite a valid assessment of a salesman's abilities but by not giving him the whole of the period stated you may give him good grounds to claim unfair dismissal. After all, he may get all the necessary orders to reach his targets in the last month of the review period. Be on the safe side and give him the benefit of the full review period. If some other more serious incident happens in the meantime or there is some clear evidence that he's sitting at home doing nothing, there will be sufficient grounds to bring forward the dismissal.

3. "How long should a review period last for?" From tribunal case law, such factors as length of service and nature of the job are the main determining factors to be balanced against the need for the company to replace with a competent or more reliable employee. Certainly nothing can be achieved by a period of less than one week; two weeks or a month would be better. A long serving employee could expect 3 to 6 months as a reasonable review period.

4. Surely, say some employers, we don't have to go through these procedures if the employee doesn't have 52 weeks' service?

48

There are various factors to look at before you can provide an answer to that question. Firstly, are you sure that the employee hasn't got 52 weeks' service? Count the weeks of service accurately, parts of a week at either end of the service count as whole weeks and if they were dismissed with pay in lieu of notice they can still add on the statutory notice requirement (1 week) to their total length of service even though they did not work it. Consequently, 49 complete weeks of actual service may be enough to claim unfair dismissal at a tribunal.

Secondly, is your disciplinary procedure a part of the contract of employment? If it has been incorporated, then by failing to follow it you are in breach of contract and have wrongfully dismissed the employee. Although he cannot take the matter of his dismissal to the industrial tribunal he can go in the usual manner to a county court alleging breach of contract. The likely damages will be determined for a period that would represent the time it would take to go though the disciplinary procedure and the appropriate period of notice. The best reason for using the disciplinary procedure with all staff regardless of service is that it is good personnel practice and shouldn't take an impossibly long time if action is promptly initiated by the first line manager.

Gross Misconduct

Finally, the example procedure shows how certain acts will be classified as gross misconduct and what action will be taken to deal with such problems.

In most organisations serious acts of misconduct are dealt with by senior management although the supervisor is often involved when the matter is discovered. Often it is how the supervisor initially handles the situation that will either help or hinder the senior manager when he comes to deal with the problem.

How do you recognise gross misconduct and what steps should the supervisor take? Actions that are considered to be gross misconduct can vary between organisations and where there are written rules these offences are often listed and classified. Even without specific rules certain conduct is almost universally treated as gross misconduct — theft, fraud, physical violence, insubordination, refusal to carry out reasonable orders, etc. These are, in fact, actions that go to the root of the contract and will destroy it. An employer cannot trust anyone who is a thief or who is likely to become violent or insubordinate.

The crucial aspect is: has the conduct destroyed the relationship between the employer and employee? There may be circumstances in which the relationship can still survive and continue in spite of obvious acts of gross misconduct on the employee's part. Many employers continue to employ people who they know are thieves because they feel that once the employee has been "fingered" he won't do it again. Alternatively, if the employee only took waste materials of little value the employer may prefer to retain his services rather than penalise him disproportionately. Perhaps his job can be rearranged so that he won't handle cash any more and so temptation won't arise.

In other words, there is a whole range of responses open to an employer so that he need not necessarily sieze the opportunity to dismiss the erring employee. One employer decided that because he had employed the lad's whole family he did not want to sour these relationships by dismissing the lad who had been caught red-handed. Another was affected by his employee's long unblemished service record which to him weighed more heavily than the £300 stolen to pay a debt. In other circumstances, dismissal has been eschewed when the employee promptly promised to pay the missing sums of money.

Similar considerations apply to most acts of gross misconduct — they can be mitigated by the circumstances and the employer does not dismiss. This has always been the case and the laws of unfair dismissal reflect this custom and practice.

The employer will always have a good reason to dismiss, without notice, any employee whom he can show fought, stole, etc., but he will also have to show that the decision was reasonable given all the surrounding circumstances, including how he investigated and put the matter to the employee to explain. Even the reliance on a written rule stating that acts of theft will result in immediate dismissal will not ensure that the employee's dismissal is automatically fair. An industrial tribunal looks at all these circumstances including consistency in enforcing such rules, the degree to which conduct is condoned, etc. The example procedure reflects this requirement. It provides for investigation, hearing the employee's version of the matter at an interview and the proper consideration of anything that might show the employee in a better light, or perhaps excuse what he has done, before a decision to dismiss is made.

Suspension During Investigation

It is often necessary to suspend an employee from work whilst an investigation is carried out. Having the chap off the premises usually ensures that bits of information trickle in that wouldn't normally do so and people won't stand around in groups waiting for the next bit of fun to break out. If the employee is told to return the next day or is subsequently instructed to return by letter or telephone after completion of the investigation, tempers have cooled and a more constructive approach can be adopted.

Does the employee have to receive pay whilst he is suspended? Sometimes it is agreed at the time of the incident that the pay will not be given but if, subsequently, the allegation is shown to be without foundation he will receive backpay. (Written procedures often have this provision.) Alternatively, the employee's written terms of employment will specify that pay is or is not given when he is suspended.

In law, there is no general right to stop the employee from working when he is willing and able, and the employer must pay him during that period of suspension unless he has given himself the right to withhold pay in the contract of employment. As a general rule of thumb it is better to pay an employee who is suspended when disciplinary matters are being investigated because withdrawal of pay is already starting to punish him before any of the facts have been determined and so presupposes his "guilt".

Suspension can also be used in a penalising way, very often as an alternative to dismissal. Sometimes, disciplinary procedures provide for a scale of short suspensions depending on the offence and its frequency. Usually the suspensions last for 2 or 3 days and are intended as a short sharp shock. Over-long periods of unpaid suspension are undesirable on two counts. It is a penalty that is inequitable: it won't affect a single man as greatly as a married man with greater financial responsibilities; additionally, it is rewarding absence from work or lateness with yet more time off work. Similarly, the practice of sending home employees who turn up impossibly late for work is not an effective control method if used too frequently.

Making the Situation Tidy

For the first line supervisor, who won't be involved in the ultimate decision, the most important contribution he can make is to ensure that the situation is tidy: provide his manager with a detailed report of the circumstances and assist with the investigation. In most cases a "tidy" situation means that the employee is suspended until an investigation can be completed and the employee is called back to work later to be interviewed, before a decision is made about his continued employment. In incidents where physical violence is used the supervisor will have to get the people concerned off the company premises as quickly as possible. It should be made clear to them that they are suspended, not dismissed. This can de-escalate the situation quite quickly. If the contestants are affected by alcohol it is even more important not to enter into long discussions but to clear them off the premises until they've sobered up. If any employee refuses to leave, a phone call to the police can usually provide the solution.

The supervisor should try to take accurate statements from those who witnessed the incident. Simply get them to relate, step by step in their own words, what they saw and heard. Make sure that sufficient detail is put in, state the time of the incident, the date, who else was there, etc., and set it all out in a written statement. Put in a little diagram of where people were standing if this will help the reader's understanding. Then pin the statements to a report outlining all facts in chronological order. An example of such a report would be:

Memo to J. Smith   From P. Davy
    General Manager   Engineering Section
                                Supervisor
                                Date June 24th

When I returned to the Engineering Department after lunch at 1.30 p.m. today I was met at the door of the workshop by R. Henry who told me that there was a fight in the stores between J. Smith and L. Pearce (both fitters grade II). They had been bickering before I went to lunch and the fight had started 3 minutes before I returned.

When I reached the store the two men had been restrained by other employees but both were very upset and angry. They were separated, Pearce went to the stores and I had Smith brought over to my office so that he could explain what had happened.

Smith said that the argument was over a lost wrench that was owned by Pearce who had accused him of stealing it. Pearce had thrown a spanner at him and said "you might as well have that bastard as well". He said that the spanner slid along the bench and dropped at Pearce's feet. It never touched him. Pearce came around the bench and started pushing Smith, threatening to thump hell out of him and blows started to be thrown. Smith said he broke away and went towards the store to get away, Pearce followed and started to hit him again. They were then restrained by other employees. Smith had bad grazes around the eyes and facial bruising but otherwise he was not seriously hurt. I instructed Smith to clock out and go home — I told him that he was suspended until tomorrow at 10.00 a.m., when he should report to the General Manager's office for a disciplinary meeting.

Next, I spoke to Pearce whose account was almost identical except he said he had not thrown the spanner at Smith, merely pushed it along the bench in disgust and it fell off the bench. Smith hadn't seen him do it but thought it had been thrown at him when he heard it strike the floor. Pearce was similarly suspended until 10.00 a.m. the next day. I went back to speak to the other employees to see who else had seen what happened. I enclose the statements of R. Turney and J. Armstrong who were present throughout the incident.

Relevant Background Information

Both the men have been involved in disagreements that have resulted in informal warnings for indiscipline and two months ago they were both given a strong talking to and their work areas separated to the farthest sides of the shop. It was not possible to arrange a transfer and neither men thought that that would be necessary once their work areas were separated.

| L. Pearce | Engaged 4/10/78 | No previous written warnings |
| J. Smith | Engaged 18/5/80 | No previous written warnings |

The use of a written report completed soon after the incident is extremely helpful later when memories have dimmed. If such an incident results in dismissal and tribunal action, it is always several months before evidence is given and references to such a document can prod the memory into action.

Action Other Than Dismissal

The example procedure makes it necessary to consider any other action that might be possible to penalise the employee rather than taking the ultimate step of dismissal. There may be quite a variety of sanctions that can be applied; generally they include demotion, transfer, loss of wages or other benefits.

Demotion

In most cases unilateral demotion of an employee would be considered a major breach of contract unless it is justified as a penultimate stage in the disciplinary procedure, i.e. after taking the normal steps to warn the employee (and give such training and assistance as necessary if the issue is job performance). This is not always an acceptable solution and the employee may prefer to be dismissed rather than return to the tools amongst employees whom he previously controlled. Sometimes it is sensible to arrange a transfer to another department or arrange another job title and a different seating arrangement or change of office so that the demotion can be seen by others as a change of responsibility, not as a stark demotion. One thing should also be considered: when will the punishment end? Will the employee never again be considered for promotion or after, say, a year of good behaviour will the individual be able to reapply for a responsible job? Such conditions should be spelt out to the employee.

Transfers

Transfers are often considered quite early in the disciplinary procedure especially where the problems relate to personality clashes or failure to cope with particular types of work. Transfer can also be used as an alternative to dismissal where it may involve moving to a less pleasant job, less opportunity to earn productivity bonuses or reduction of basic wage rate, etc. Removal from friends and associates are all part of the punitive effect.

Similarly, some thought should be given to when the employee will be "brought in from the cold" and be able to resume the previous job.

Termination of Employment

Alternative action other than dismissal is not always possible, especially in smaller concerns, and dismissal is the only feasible option. The example procedure defines the circumstances in which notice is given or not given to end the contract of employment. If the warning procedure has been completed then notice must be given.

It is important to note that notice should not run concurrently with a review period, i.e. "you are given four weeks' notice of dismissal and during this time you must improve your attendance and timekeeping. If you reach an acceptable standard your notice of dismissal will be withdrawn". Notice of dismissal cannot be withdrawn unilaterally and the employee may not accept the withdrawal and leave anyway — claiming unfair dismissal. Giving notice of dismissal under the guise of a warning is not a fair procedure — the warning procedure has to be completed before notice is given; consequently there is quite a possibility that a tribunal would find such a dismissal unfair.

The Formal Disciplinary Interview

Once the informal level has been passed, more senior managers usually become involved in the disciplinary action although the first line manager still has a role to play. It is a good idea to discuss the problems with a departmental manager even if your company procedure allows the immediate supervisor to give the first written warning. Often the procedure requires the personnel department to be involved once the formal stage is reached; some even require the personnel officer to conduct the interview and give the warning. Clearly procedures have tremendous variety but in all of them the immediate supervisor will greatly assist if he prepares a simple written report outlining the problems and the action he has taken so far. If it is a serious matter that is going straight into the formal procedure, with no previous informal action having been taken, the report will outline the incident and how the situation was "tidied up". If the warning has been given then he usually has the responsibility of monitoring progress. Therefore, involvement in the interview is important just so that he knows what the position is.

The formal disciplinary interview itself will not vary greatly from the informal disciplinary interview. The aims and ways of going about it remain the same but there are features and considerations which come out more strongly at this level.

Calling the Meeting

When the employee is called to the meeting, sometimes this is done by letter. A clear outline of what allegations or complaints he is to face should be given. The date and venue should be given as should details of who will be in attendance.

If it is a very serious matter that is likely to end in dismissal, there is no harm in pointing this out, e.g. dismissal is to be considered unless he is able to provide an adequate explanation of the situation or mitigating circumstances.

It is not unknown for employees to resign or not turn up to such an interview because they know they have no adequate explanation or mitigating factors to help them.

If the employee does not turn up, an explanation for his non-attendance should be sought, perhaps a new date set, and the warning given that if he does not turn up again (without adequate reason) his dismissal will be effected.

Minutes

It is sensible for the person conducting the interview to take notes of the conversation. This is particularly important if it is an issue involving gross misconduct. Include any answers or explanations that the employee might give. These notes will form the basis of the written warning. Sometimes the manager may feel that it is necessary to take a tape-recording of the situation. Ideally, this should not be done without the employee knowing that he is going down on tape. From the point of unfair dismissal actions it is very rare for tribunals to admit recordings as evidence and they will usually only do so when it was known by all the participants at the time that a tape-recording was being made.

Witnesses to the Interview

Does there have to be a witness present? It is not essential but a secretary taking notes is very useful. The employee may wish to be accompanied by a colleague or a recognised union representative and in that case the presence of someone else on the management team would be sensible.

Witnesses

At the formal stages it is more likely that witnesses will have to be introduced into the meeting because more serious disciplinary incidents are involved. It is sufficient to relate precisely to the employee what has been discovered about the incident and that there are witnesses to support this view. If the employee does not challenge this view and accepts that these are essentially the true facts of the situation, there is no need to involve witnesses. If a challenge is made to any of the facts it is essential that the witness is brought to the meeting and asked to repeat again his previous statements. They may have given signed statements but if the recalcitrant employee is adamant and his version of the facts is feasible then he must have the chance to question those who have made allegations against him. Additionally, this helps management, because unless you see both employees together you have little opportunity to really assess who is telling the truth.

This shouldn't be an opportunity for an argument or confrontation between the two people involved. Keep the proceedings to recounting what the witness saw and answering questions from the accused employee.

Sometimes the allegations come from customers or business associates who would not be prepared to attend. In this case some form of written statement will have to suffice. The employee should be shown a copy of any such statement. If the employee challenges the accuracy of the allegation then the employer must tactfully put the explanation to the customer or business associate and see what reply is given. In the end the employer must decide who he believes.

Investigation

Very often managers are faced with two completely different tales, quite persuasively put to them; so what happens then? There may be no conclusive evidence one way or the other. However, the impression can be formed that one set of events is more likely to be true than another. Knowing the recalcitrant employee, the veracity of the witness, etc., in these circumstances the employer must be able to show that he carried out all the investigation that he could be reasonably expected to carry out. Don't be thrown by these events. Adjourn the proceedings to check out the stories and decide if other relevant investigations could be made to get corroboration for one side or the other. (This situation can happen quite frequently if disciplinary action has been initiated without proper investigation beforehand and the adjournment will help to repair the situation without any loss of face.) When investigations are complete the interviewing manager must decide which version of the facts he believes and why; not which version of the facts has been proved beyond all reasonable doubt. It is not a High Court standard of proof you are looking for.

An employer cannot investigate too thoroughly: in fact it is his insurance. If, after the dismissal, it turns out that new evidence shows that the employee was not to blame or the county court does not convict for theft, etc., it will not rebound on to the employer's head at an industrial tribunal if the investigation was rigorous. It may seem very unfair that the person has been penalised for something that could not be proven or that he did not do. However, the employer's defence will be that "at the time the decision was made, after extensive investigation, I had reasonable grounds to believe that the employee was responsible". All things being equal, this should be sufficient defence (see page 78 for further discussion of dismissal for theft).

If the investigation supports the employee's story or puts the allegations in too much doubt then quash the proceedings immediately; you will not lose face — it is the right thing to do.

Shop Stewards

Another problem of which managers must be aware is that any formal disciplinary action taken against a recognised shop steward ought to be delayed until the ACAS Code of Practice recommendations can be followed, i.e. the matter should be discussed with the convenor or the full-time union official.

This recognises the industrial relations dimension of the problem and should not be seen as an attempt to treat them differently or apply different standards of behaviour or job performance. Disciplinary action taken against a recognised shop steward is often seen as an attack on the union and

58

frequently results in industrial action being taken in his support. It is sensible to clear the path before action is taken.

How to Give a Written Warning

The interview that precedes the confirmed written warning will follow the same overall pattern of the informal disciplinary interview:

- make sure that the setting is comfortable and that adequate seating is available. Interruptions by telephone should be prevented and a "do not disturb" sign on the door will also help. Keep the approach formal but friendly. Make sure that noise levels are not excessive;

- don't lose your temper or raise your voice and observe all the usual social courtesies. See page 29 for other useful hints;

- ask the employee if he wishes any colleague or his recognised trade union representative to accompany him;

- since he has already been informed of the purpose of the meeting it would be quite permissible to launch straight in and ask for his explanation but a better tactic when dealing with non-gross misconduct issues is to summarise the steps that have been taken to date, to discuss, assist and warn the employee about his conduct or job performance, asking him at each point whether he agrees that this has happened. If standards are still unacceptable, show him the documentary evidence, if any, and ask him what he makes of it. Ask him does he think he has improved and has he really tried to make an effort. Try and get the two-way conversation going from the outset. Ask him if there is any explanation for the failure to improve. Search for possible reasons and if some personal problems seem to be at the back of it consider if there is any action that the company can take to assist (it may not have been done very effectively at the informal stage or subsequent problems may have occurred). Explain to the employee that, although feeling sympathetic to any personal difficulties, the warning procedure will continue and eventually he will be dismissed. Evaluate any reasons/excuses given by the employee;

- once again, specify time limits for improvement and indicate that the improvement must be consistently maintained. Set clear standards of job performance to be attained;

- explain that the warning is a first (or second formal or final) written warning and written confirmation will be given later, based on the notes of the meeting;
- make it clear what the next step in the procedure will be if standards are not met or the incident of misconduct occurs again;
- tell the employee that if he is dissatisfied about the disciplinary action taken against him he can appeal. Specify what the appeal procedure is.

Checklist: Formal Disciplinary Interview

Preliminary Steps

1. Make sure you have all the relevant facts available including any appropriate documents and other written data.
2. Define precisely what the complaint is, i.e. is it a breach of the company's till procedures or an allegation of taking money from the till? (the former might be the better approach if hard evidence of theft is hard to find).
3. Consider what excuses might be offered and check them out beforehand.
4. Confirm by letter the purpose of the disciplinary meeting or explain verbally to the employee beforehand what the interview is about. If it is a complex issue involving documentation, it is useful to give copies in advance or else you will have to adjourn the meeting to allow the employee to study the documentation and provide some explanation.
5. Make notes of the matters you intend to raise so that you do not leave anything out.
6. Arrange a witness of the proceedings to be present. It is useful if notes can be taken.
7. Inform the employee of his right to be accompanied by a colleague or recognised trade union representative.
8. Should witnesses to the incidents be required, can you round them up at short notice to attend the meeting?
9. If the employee to be disciplined is a recognised shop steward, has the convenor or full-time official been consulted before action is taken?

Procedure

1. Recap on previous disciplinary action taken for the offence or failure to meet standards and restate the problem. Do not

jump to conclusions and start thinking of the penalties; satisfy yourself that the employee is at fault.

2. Ask is there any explanation to account for the failure to improve or for the recurrence of the misconduct. Evaluate the reasons given:

   (a) Is the employee entirely at fault or was someone else responsible? Was it an organisational failure outside his control?

   (b) If it was the employee's fault, are there any personal or other mitigating circumstances to be taken into account?

   (c) Are the explanations just excuses? If so make it clear you do not accept them.

3. If the employee has provided an adequate explanation or there is no real shred of evidence to support the allegation, do not be afraid to quash the proceedings then and there.

4. If evidence is a little thin on the ground but there is some merit in the allegation, reopen the investigation after adjourning the meeting. Always check out contended facts again.

5. Decide on the balance of probabilities what version of the facts is true.

6. Tell the employee your decision and then consider with the employee —

   (a) what action can be taken to help solve the problem, i.e. retraining, transfer to a different department (even in conduct cases this may be useful);

   (b) what penalty should be given, e.g. first written warning or, if the matter is serious, a final written warning (if your company procedure allows this flexibility);

   (c) clear targets or performance standards, or specify what is expected of the employee;

   (d) decide on a review period, if appropriate, when the matter will be assessed;

   (e) indicate what the next stage in the procedure is if the assessment is unfavourable or the act of misconduct is committed again (follow what is specified in your company procedure);

7. Explain the appeals procedure if the employee is unhappy about the disciplinary action.

8. Make sure a letter is given/sent to the employee outlining the substance of the interview.

Final Written Warnings and Dismissal

When coming to the end of the disciplinary procedure, a final warning must be given stating unequivocally that a repeat of the misconduct or failure to improve after a reasonable period of review will result in dismissal, with the appropriate contractual notice being given. Don't water it down to make it sound nice, i.e. "liable to be dismissed" or "may be dismissed". Such a warning must be confirmed in writing to the employee after the disciplinary meeting. When the situation is reviewed again and there has been no improvement or there has been a repeat of the misconduct that was the subject of previous warnings, another interview must be convened to take action to dismiss the employee. Never dismiss by letter, always try to see the employee first.

Checklist Part 1: Dismissal After Warning

1. Is dismissal being effected at the expiry of the review period and has performance or conduct been unsatisfactory?

2. Is it a repeat of an act of misconduct for which a final warning has been previously given? If so, is it a reasonable period of time since the warning was given, considering the nature of the offence and any lifetime limit to the warning?

3. Can the employee give any mitigating circumstances that ought to be considered?

4. Is there any other penalty short of dismissal that is feasible?

5. Decide whether or not you require notice to be worked.

6. Inform the employee at the interview of the appeal procedure.

7. Confirm dismissal, notice arrangements, any other pay to come, and other termination instructions in a letter.

8. If written reasons for dismissal are requested by the employee or required to be given by your company's disciplinary procedure, write giving full details of the reason for dismissal, the stages of warning gone through and enclose copies of previous written warnings.

Checklist Part 2: Dismissal for Gross Misconduct

1. Has the employee been brought back from suspension for a disciplinary interview?
2. Are you satisfied that on reasonable grounds, after full investigation, the employee was at fault and to blame? Did the employee know that breach of the rule or particular act of misconduct would be treated as gross misconduct? Ignorance is no defence if he might reasonably be expected to know.
3. Has the employee had the opportunity to state his case?
4. Consistency: has dismissal always been the penalty attached to the breach of the rules or the act of gross misconduct, or have there been different solutions in the past? If so, why was there a departure from the normal penalty on previous occasions? If the circumstances are the same now, you will also have to consider a similar lesser penalty.
5. Are there any mitigating circumstances that ought to be taken into consideration?
6. Is there any lesser penalty that can be used in this situation?

Note

Once it has been decided that dismissal action will be taken for gross misconduct, the employee should not work out notice except in very rare circumstances. There is also no liability to give pay in lieu of notice though many employers do so as an ex gratia payment. Additionally, all payments earned up to the date of dismissal should be paid including accrued holiday pay, unless there is any contractual term that allows accrued holiday payments not to be paid. Companies under wages orders all have the right to withhold accrued holiday pay providing the employee is told that he is being dismissed for gross misconduct.

Written Reasons

Written reasons must be provided within 14 days of the employee's request (either orally or in writing), detailing exactly the reasons for dismissal, providing the employee has at least 26 weeks' service. It would, though, be good personnel practice to comply with such a request regardless of the length of service.

Some company disciplinary procedures require reasons to be given in writing automatically even if the employee does not make the request. The statement must be in writing (it is sensible to send it by recorded delivery) and there must be sufficiently detailed information contained in it to make the situation clear to any interested party. If previous correspondence exists, i.e. warning letters, dismissal letters, etc., it is a good idea to attach them as well.

It is a most important document because it is admissible in any unfair dismissal hearing, so take care in its drafting.

Example: Written Reasons for Dismissal

Dear Mr. Dodds,

Further to your request for written reasons for dismissal we would confirm that the reason was your lack of capability to perform your job reliably because of your addiction to alcohol.

As you are aware, the situation has been the subject of several meetings over the past eighteen months. We enclose the letters sent to you after each meeting.

The matter came to our attention because your attendance and timekeeping had begun to deteriorate very badly. During the meeting your underlying drink problem was discussed and, as a result of a visit to the company doctor, you were given one month's leave to take remedial treatment.

When you returned to work we had restructured your job as contracts manager to remove some of the duties that you had previously carried out. However, against our advice, you requested a return to all your previous duties including site visiting. We did not feel that this would give you any real chance to stay on the wagon but we agreed because you had improved so much.

By June this year it was clear that the same timekeeping and attendance problems were arising again. You were told that we were prepared to allow you further time off to dry out, providing your job could be restructured before you returned. However, you refused this suggestion. You were placed under final warning with a one month review period and during that time the situation did not improve. Following a final meeting, you were therefore dismissed.

Practical Application

Having looked in general outline at how to operate a disciplinary procedure effectively we now turn to some specific problem areas that occur over and over again.

None of the solutions or strategies are the only ones that can be used. In every day situations, responding with flexibility and not a little creativeness will always be necessary. Mostly, the solutions err on the side of caution, and heavily reflect the industrial tribunal case law that has grown up over the years. Some of the problems covered are not really disciplinary problems at all (e.g. ill health dismissals) but there are aspects of procedural correctness which will be of interest to anyone who manages staff, and that's why they have been included. The chapter is divided into three sections:

(a) Minor misconduct including lateness, absenteeism, poor job performance.

(b) Gross misconduct including theft, fighting.

(c) Other problems including office romances and misconduct outside work.

Minor Misconduct

Lateness

Most employees are required to attend for work at specific times and are expected, with the exception of tea and meal breaks, to remain at work until the allotted finishing time. These arrangements must be specified in their contract of employment. A variety of standards of strictness exist. In some cases, three mintues' grace is allowed before an employee is counted as late and money deducted from the paypacket; additionally, they must go to their immediate supervisor and get his permission to start work and get their clockcard signed. In other instances things are not nearly so well defined and very often arrangements exist for flexible starting times either in a formal flexi-time system or as an unofficial nodded-to piece of custom or practice. Whatever the standards applied, the employer must make sure his standards are known to his employees. Alternatively, when advantage is being taken, he must be prepared to draw the line. This is where the immediate supervisor is so important to tackle the lateness syndrome before it becomes an unshakeable habit.

It should be regular practice for supervisors to query the reason why employees are late: even check out these reasons if they seem tenuous. New employees joining the company should be told about the standard of timekeeping expected of them and that they must present an explanation when they are late. It is often a good idea to get employees to telephone en route if they are going to be late.

Procedures like this reinforce the habit of good timekeeping and emphasise that good timekeeping is all part of putting in a credible job performance. If they are the kind of person to whom time has little relevance, they will probably leave and go elsewhere. However, good timekeepers can deteriorate to the extent that they need to be told and this is where the informal disciplinary interview can help.

From the outset you will need to know the answers to the following questions before you can approach the employee concerned and effectively carry out an interview. For instance, are you picking on a troublemaker? If you are then there may be some consistency problems. What are the timekeeping records of other staff? A little investigation may show that their performance is no worse than a lot of others — they will have to be dealt with in the same way.

A good start is a general memo or note in the wage packet pointing out deteriorating standards of timekeeping. Give some indication of an acceptable standard, i.e. once a week but for a good reason. Point out that transport problems can usually be solved by getting up earlier and catching the earlier bus or train, etc. Point out that it is their responsibility to get to work on time. Detail the procedure to be adopted if they arrive late. Remind them that permission must be obtained in advance to take time off work. Indicate that this is a toughening up or returning to previously good standards and that normal disciplinary action will be taken against employees failing to come up to standard. Don't forget to be constructive as well; suggest that anyone with problems over prompt attendance at work should speak to their supervisor or personnel officer. (Very often several employees are affected by a poor bus service and the company could quite usefully take the matter up on their behalf, especially if other employers in the area have the same problem.) Such general warnings do not count as a first warning to an individual who is being disciplined. It is a scene setter.

Are there any accurate records of timekeeping, i.e. clockcards, signing book, etc? In many organisations there are not, so the next step must be a monitoring of everyone's attendance for 2 or 3 weeks before speaking to them. Don't snoop. Tell them what you are doing. The purpose is to correct the behaviour not to silently and secretly build up a case against them and thump them over the head with it. If they manage to improve for two weeks, knowing that their timekeeping is being watched, it is possible that the improvement will continue afterwards.

Now you should be sufficiently set up with the facts to go ahead with an informal interview if any employee is still falling below standard. (See page 25 on informal warnings.) Simply set out to the employee what the complaint is and ask him to explain why there has been this deterioration in timekeeping. These reasons will revolve around two areas:

(a) actual reasons that make it impossible to attend work on time — i.e. a sick aged parent who needs attention in the morning, poor public transport facilities, taking children to school; or

(b) the usual malaise i.e. can't get up in the morning because the alarm clock's broken.

Both areas ought to be explored thoroughly, particularly as the latter is often a euphemism for not liking to work with a particular person or doing a particular job. Even a general health problem can be disguised here. See if there are any solutions that present themselves. Can hours of work be varied to cope with a temporary problem? Are there any other sources of help which you can give the employee information about? Local authorities often keep lists of approved childminders who frequently look after children in emergency situations. It is often useful to keep information like this for future reference.

Try and talk the employees through the problem so that they realise they must make other arrangements to cope with their personal circumstances (what about neighbours, other members of the family, etc?) because the stage is being reached where formal disciplinary action will have to be taken.

This kind of constructive approach — joint problem solving — has got to be better then bashing people over the head with written warnings!

If there is an underlying health problem encourage the employee to go to his doctor or use the company doctor. With young employees it is usually the fact that they are not used to the routine of work and need to be eased into it and establish good attendance habits. Arranging a pick-up by another employee can often provide the "knock-up" routine and incentive that is needed. Don't forget to tell the employee that the interview counts as the informal stage of the disciplinary procedure and say that the matter will be reviewed. Remind the employee that consideration for his genuine problems must be balanced against the company's needs for employees to attend work promptly.

Even if warnings have to be issued later and finally dismissal itself, the ground is completely prepared and the employer will have acted reasonably given all the circumstances. (The cynical will say that you have helped to sabotage those sympathy factors that so often wreck the employer's defence to alleged unfair dismissal at tribunal.)

If there is no response to this informal warning or there is an improvement for a short time and then it deteriorates it will be time to start formal warnings (see page 39).

Example Warning Letter: First Written Warning

Dear Mr. Evans,

In spite of your supervisor's informal conversations about your poor timekeeping both at the commencement of work and at the lunch time break, the lack of improvement made it necessary to hold a formal disciplinary meeting on May 14th. This letter is confirmation of the disciplinary action taken against you.

Between March and the beginning of May this year you have been late on average twice a week and late back from lunch a similar number of times (a copy of the records was shown to you). There doesn't appear to be any underlying cause for your poor attendance except, as you admitted, you find it difficult to wake up in the mornings. Your reason for late returns to work in the lunch hour is that you occasionally go home for lunch and are often delayed by the traffic. It was explained to you that only one hour was given for lunch and if it is not possible for you to complete lunch arrangements within that time you should change those arrangements. As you know, canteen facilities are provided.

At the interview your departmental manager stated that in future you must ensure that:

(a) you clock in at 8.30 a.m. each working day. Only 3 minutes grace is allowed;

(b) if you are late you must report directly to your supervisor with a full explanation;

(c) as stated in your terms and conditions statement, if you are going to be absent from work you telephone or arrange a message to be received by your supervisor no later than 10 a.m. on the same day. It is quite impossible to organise production schedules adequately if you do not contact promptly;

(d) return promptly from your lunch break each day.

The company does expect high standards of timekeeping. If you cannot maintain these standards over the review period we agreed, i.e. one month, further disciplinary action will be taken against you. This will be in the form of a final warning, which if unheeded will result in your dismissal.

If you are dissatisfied with the disciplinary action taken against you an appeals procedure is outlined in your contract of employment.

Example: Final Written Warning

Dear Mr. Evans,
Re Disciplinary Meeting June 16th
It is a matter of great concern to both your departmental manager and myself that it has been necessary yet again to bring to your attention the necessity for good timekeeping.

The disciplinary meeting on May 14th recorded your first written warning and outlined precisely what was required of you. However, there has been no improvement in your timekeeping (see copy of record card enclosed) during the review period. I understand that you do not wish to give up your practice of going home at lunchtimes, so running the risk that you will be late if you are caught in the traffic. You also do not know why you are unable to reach the factory on time in the mornings. By all accounts you are perfectly healthy and concerned to keep your job.

It must now be quite clear to you that your poor timekeeping will result in your dismissal.

I have no alternative but to confirm your Department Manager's warning that unless there is an immediate and sustained improvement in your timekeeping both at the start of work and at the lunch break you will be given notice of dismissal.

The matter will be reviewed again in one month's time and I sincerely hope that you will take this warning to heart and make the necessary effort to improve your timekeeping.

If you are dissatisfied with the disciplinary action taken against you an appeals procedure is outlined in your contract of employment.

Checklist

1. State precisely the nature of the complaint: what, when.
2. Refer to company rules if relevant and state why conduct is not acceptable.
3. Refer to excuses given if relevant and why they have not been accepted.
4. State precisely what the employee should do to remedy the situation; what help he will receive in the way of retraining, etc.
5. Set a date for reviewing the situation.
6. State what will happen if there has been no improvement or the conduct is repeated again. Specifically relate this action to the company's disciplinary procedure.
7. Inform employee about appeal procedure.

Absenteeism

Every employer views absenteeism as an awkward problem to cure and there can be difficulties in sorting out an appropriate procedure to deal with it.

Contracts of employment usually specify the hours and days of work and the employee has to ask permission if he wishes to take time off, to have holidays according to his entitlement or for any other reason. The employer may or may not give his permission. Other spells of absence may be caused by illness, injury (with or without a medical certificate) or exercising some statutory right such as time off for antenatal care, trade union duties, public duties, etc. Other spells of absence are unapproved and without contractual sanction.

Like lateness, different standards are tolerated in different organisations and different policies adopted as regards pay for these absences. In 1983 a new statutory sick pay scheme will be introduced and it will become extremely important for accurate records of spells of ill health/injury absence to be kept, if this is not already being done. Statutory rights like time off for antenatal care and trade union duties must be with pay whilst time off for public duties is without pay. Holiday entitlement is usually specified in the contract of employment but other situations arise where extended leave of absence is given for compassionate reasons or for holidays abroad. Permission may also be given for Territorial Army duties, religious observance, etc.

What days count?
When a poor absence record is being assessed which days should be counted and which days should be ignored? Clearly, any day when prior permission was given for the absence should not be counted. Neither should periods of certificated sick leave — the uncertificated periods are more debatable but if the employee wasn't challenged at the time it is safer to assume that they are genuine. The only days that are left are those of unapproved absence, and it is these days that form the basis for the complaint against the employee. As most employees can trot out a convincing account of a bilious attack or a bout of food poisoning, it is better to adopt the tack of reliability rather than complain about the rather limited incidents of unapproved absence or the extremely contestable area of uncertificated absence. Additionally, many doctors in the future will not be signing sick notes during the first week of absence, which could mean the dispute area will broaden. A proper system of self-certification ought to be drawn up.

Using this approach all absence that has not received management approval, whether you consider it genuine or not, can count if you slant your complaint to one of unreliability. There's no question of arguing over the authenticity of sick notes, whether or not the doctor dishes them out like confetti. It can all be genuine but it will all add up, together with the unapproved absence, to show the appalling attendance record of an unreliable employee and warnings can therefore be given on that basis. Such a strategy takes the heat out of the situation; you are not calling anyone a liar and you can rely on the usual defence, "the needs of the business, in this case for reliable employees".

The informal procedure to combat absenteeism is much the same as for lateness. Make sure employees are asked why they are absent and examine these reasons closely. There should be a clear understanding about the acceptable level of absence by both managers and employees. Ensure that there are procedures (very often they are written into the contract of employment) to specify notification by a given time on the first day of absence, when sick notes must be sent, the requirement to keep the company informed of progress, etc. Failure to follow these procedures can in themselves form sufficient reason to give warning and eventually to dismiss if they are seriously flouted.

Now that the complaint has been defined it is possible to have an informal disciplinary interview (see page 29).

Set out the complaint, namely that they are unreliable and show them the documentary evidence of their attendance pattern. Sometimes this comes as a surprise to employees because they live one week at a time and do not actually add those days they have off together and realise that their attendance is poor. Point out that you accept that some or all of the absence appears to be genuine but the problem remains for the company to have employees at work.

Example: First Written Warning

Dear Mrs. Jones,

Over a month ago your supervisor spoke to you about your increasingly poor attendance record. Since the beginning of the year you have had 28 certificated and uncertificated days absence, and three unapproved days for which there was no recorded reason. On several occasions you failed to follow the proper procedure to inform your supervisor of your absence by 10 a.m. on the first day, which caused all kinds of problems in getting the company's weekly wages calculated on time.

There has been no improvement since your supervisor spoke to you, because a further 5 days absence was recorded last month and as a result a formal disciplinary interview was held on November 24th. This letter is confirmation of the disciplinary action taken at that meeting.

Arising from that meeting we are in no doubt that your absences are caused by genuine health and personal problems with which we sympathise and hope you will resolve. We are glad that you have accepted our suggestion to visit the company doctor, we feel sure that he will assist you.

We confirm that you will be taking one week's leave of absence at half pay next week to attend to court matters.

Your departmental manager confirmed at the meeting that you must conform to the company's normal notification procedure when you are absent (a copy of your contract was given to you detailing the procedure). You are a key employee and when you are away an immediate stand-in must be sought, so please give us as much warning as possible.

Additionally, we were at pains to point out that because of the nature of your job, reliability is very crucial and unless the situation improves to, say, two days average loss of attendance per month, we will have to consider replacing you.

You have agreed that the company should contact your doctor and we will await further information from him before we decide what to do.

Comment

Once again, start probing for reasons, very often there is a sorry tale of personal problems that affect health, etc. Try to encourage the employee to go to the doctor or see the company doctor. Are there any outside bodies, i.e. voluntary organisations or local government departments that can help with the personal problems? Is there any action the company can take, e.g. vary days of work or reduce the number of days temporarily; give leave of absence to sort things out, etc? Very often poor attendance records are associated with alcoholism; perhaps the company can give time off to help the employee dry out. If intermittent illness is caused by an underlying medical problem perhaps the company doctor can get things moving for a remedial operation.

It may be a good idea to ask the employee for permission for the company to get a report from his doctor to see precisely what the problem is and the likelihood of it being sorted out by an operation or other treatment.

Get into a frank, open relationship with the employee from the start. You really won't know what the problem is until you ask and there may be some extremely useful things you can do to help. Even if eventual dismissal is the outcome, one ex-employee will be saying around the neighbourhood that the ' company tried to help, but it was understandable that they could not put up with the absences for ever. If the employee won't discuss any explanations for his poor attendance then he should be told that in that case nothing can be taken into account and you can only decide what to do on the basis of the facts you know. Set a period to review the situation (anything less than a month would be pointless) and say that if things do not improve during that time a formal written warning will be given.

If there has been a persistent breach of procedure the employee must be told precisely what is expected of him and if it is a contractual procedure then arguably it should be treated at the formal disciplinary level from the outset.

Example: Final Written Warning

Dear Mrs. Jones,

Further to our previous meeting last month we are now in receipt of your doctor's report which confirms all that you told us and indicates that he has changed your course of treatment of which he has high hopes.

Your departmental manager has told you that we are prepared to wait a further month to review your attendance at work but regrettably we will not be able to retain you in employment any longer unless there are signs of a distinct improvement. As he told you, we have looked at the possibility of transferring you to another job where good attendance is not so crucial and paying you on a daily attendance basis. It has not been possible for us to find such a vacancy at present but one may become available over the next month and if it does we shall offer it to you on the basis described.

We are pleased to note that you have been prompt in your notification of absence since our last meeting.

Comment

You will note that the letters drop the strict disciplinary approach once it is conceded that there are genuine medical problems and it is clear that the unauthorised absence is because of family commitments. In general, the "reliability" approach is not concerned to dispense blame but to ensure that the employee knows how much absence can be tolerated, depending on the needs of the business.

Once again, if an improvement is not forthcoming the employee should be interviewed to make sure there is no other relevant change to his or her situation that may have a bearing on his ability to improve attendance. In this case, also to confirm if alternative employment can be arranged and if the employee is prepared to accept it. (There is no obligation to create a job.) Otherwise, notice of dismissal may have to be given.

Poor Performance in Carrying Out Duties

There are certain problems that immediately stand out when job performance is being discussed.

1. What do you mean by poor performance? Not enough sales? Not enough profitable sales; not enough new business; poor coverage of existing customers to sell the company's extended product range? Is he failing to keep proper records and account for his movements? Are there sales targets?
2. Is it quality or quantity? Are there individual production targets or wastage figures showing the percentage of rejects?
3. Is it a lack of innate ability or is he just not wanting to do the job properly?

You must define exactly what the complaint is and what you think the employee should be capable of, otherwise you cannot begin to discipline the employee. You must be able to quantify the standard required. Sometimes, the standards required are largely subjective, i.e. the dental receptionist with the unpleasant off-hand manner, so you have to describe the standards that are required. Sometimes it is the inability of the individual to organise the work, to work to time limits, to work without supervision, and, at more senior levels, to initiate appropriate action.

Once you have decided what the complaint is about, waste no more time. Check your company's disciplinary procedure to see what the appropriate level of disciplinary action is. In some cases, salesmen failing to reach targets may go straight to the formal disciplinary levels. Start informal disciplinary action (see page 25).

The usual pattern of the disciplinary interview is still applicable to this kind of problem:

(a) explain the complaint in detail, suggest the reasons why the employee is going wrong, and ask if there are any special reasons why they have been unable to reach the required standards. Make sure they know what the standards are;

(b) listen to and evaluate any reasons they might give;

(c) consider what help can be given to the employee, e.g. retraining, extra attention — sitting by Nellie — a transfer to a different job;

(d) make it absolutely clear what is expected of them in the most basic terms and, if there are problems, who to go to for help. Set reasonably attainable targets with the employee;

(e) point out that this is an informal warning and if there is no improvement over a reasonable period of time further disciplinary action will be taken. Remember to explain the appeals procedure.

Failure to secure a better performance at the informal level must mean that formal action must be initiated (see page 39).

Example: First Written Warning

Dear Mr. Kelly,

Your sales manager had a long discussion with you last Friday about your failure to consistently meet the minimum sales target which is laid down in your letter of engagement. He has subsequently asked me to confirm the first formal warning which he gave to you.

At the meeting you could give no reason for your poor performance but suggested that your generally low state of health may be to blame. The sales manager believes that your low state of motivation and application to work is largely to blame. It was arranged that you should have a medical with the company doctor to see if there are any problems.

I must re-emphasise that the minimum target figure must be reached every month otherwise it is not in the company's financial interest to employ you. In any future month that you fail to obtain the minimum standard you will be given a final warning which, if unheeded, will result in your dismissal.

If you are dissatisfied with the disciplinary action taken against you, you may appeal in writing, setting out your reasons, to the sales director.

Example: Final Written Warning

Dear Mr. Kelly,

This letter confirms the warning given to you at the disciplinary meeting yesterday. As you are well aware your job as sales representative is a performance orientated job and your performance in that job is measured by the sales you achieve and the amount of new business you obtain. These requirements were laid down in your letter of appointment dated May 25th last year:

"You will be required to achieve a minimum sales target of £20,000 per month (periodically revised) and actively secure new customers at the rate of 4 per month. The company will supply most of your leads. Failure to reach these requirements will result in dismissal".

Our discussion yesterday ranged through all the explanations you gave for your poor performance.

You said:

1. The products were not competitive enough and were unfavourably priced compared to our northern competitor. This you agreed could not be true after you read the recently commissioned marketing report which showed that our share of the market was increasing all over the country compared to our northern competitor. Certainly it is against the experience reported by our other salesmen, none of whom have fallen below the minimum requirement.

2. Your territory was not very good because it is the smallest one: as you are aware the territories are established on the basis of a computor analysis not on the size of physical area covered. Your territory contains as many medium and large sized companies as other representatives with much larger territories.

3. Insufficient leads: this you agreed was not true once the figures were checked with the sales manager.
4. You took two weeks holiday during the assessment month: it was demonstrated to you that standing re-orders would account for at least half of your minimum target and it was quite possible for you to have made up the other £10,000 in the remaining two weeks. This is a minimum sales target, all other salesmen get considerably more.

We did however agree with you that a fluke result may have occurred that month and therefore we decided that you should have the benefit of the doubt and a further month to see if you can maintain your target.

Failure to do so will result in your dismissal.

Gross Misconduct

Theft

On page 49 we outlined the concept of gross misconduct of which theft is an example. It is important for the employer to realise what pitfalls there are in dealing with this type of disciplinary problem.

There are three main areas to handle properly: investigation: the right to explain: reasonable decision to dismiss considering all the circumstances.

As we have already observed, stealing from the employer would generally be accepted by everyone as an act of gross misconduct, but employers must still investigate properly.

Investigation

Investigate your suspicions: what has gone wrong? Are there accurate records available, till rolls, receipt books, stock records, etc? Precisely what evidence have you got that points the finger at a particular employee? If the employee was caught red-handed, who saw what happened and do their allegations hang together? Does the evidence that you have accumulated allow you to have:

(i) reasonable grounds for thinking the employee was acting dishonestly, i.e. no other explanation for the conduct;

(ii) covered all reasonable areas that would repay investigation to support that contention;

(iii) a reasonable belief that the employee was acting dishonestly.

Merely suspecting the employee is not sufficient grounds to dismiss, but a reasonable belief after proper investigation is. If it is not possible to say that on reasonable grounds you believe your employee was acting dishonestly, can you prove disobedience by the employee, e.g. failure to follow till rules, flagrant breach of documentary procedures, etc?

Right to explain

Once the investigation has been completed the employee must be interviewed and told what the employer thinks the facts are, and be given the chance to explain. Very often employees suspected are involved in the earlier investigation but when it is decided that action should be taken, a separate disciplinary interview should be held. Evaluate the explanations given. Do they hold water? If the facts are contested, opportunity should be given to question witnesses (see page 57).

There may be problems in getting hold of the employee. Very often the police have been called in and he has been spirited away and charged. Write to his home (or to his representative, the solicitor) explaining that you wish the employee to attend an interview (give time and date) to explain his behaviour. Alternatively he or his solicitor may make written representations with regard to his behaviour, or present any mitigating circumstances before any decision is made to dismiss him. Point out that if the employee does not attend or give a written reply, the decision will be made on the facts to hand and he will be informed.

Reasonable decision to dismiss considering all the circumstances

Once the employee's explanations have been given the employer must decide whether this act of misconduct irreparably damages the relationship with the employee so that there ceases to be a position of trust between them. Such things as previously condoning the action, long service which up to now has been unblemished, the possibility of transferring the employee to a job where money won't be handled, etc. may have a bearing on this.

Do you have to wait until the matter comes to court?

In short the answer is no; the employer only has to believe on reasonable grounds, after adequate investigation, that the employee has acted dishonestly and he is as likely to believe that at the time the incident occurs as he is after waiting three or four months until the case is heard. The court has to decide the case on the basis that it is proven 'beyond all reasonable doubt' and there are many technicalities which can cause the charges to be quashed. If the employer decides to suspend (either with or without pay) he will have to allow the employee to resume work when, for instance, the substance of the acquittal was that the police failed to caution the employee properly! It is probably more sensible to dismiss immediately following the investigation and meeting with the employee.

Often the interview will be adjourned so that the employer can consider what action to take. When the employee is recalled he can be told of the decision. Confirm that decision in writing. Don't forget to tell the employee about the company's appeal procedure.

Fighting and Physical Assault

The general procedure to be adopted when cases of violence break out can follow the following general headings:

(a) inform senior managers as soon as possible and take action to quell the disorder;

(b) suspend those involved until an investigation can be completed and tell them they will be recalled for a disciplinary interview, when a decision will be made about their continued employment. Management must avoid taking precipitate action to dismiss until all the facts are to hand;

(c) complete investigation of others who have witnessed the incident. Very often it is a good idea for a manager to visit the suspended employees at their homes so they can recount what happened. Take statements from those involved;

(d) hold a disciplinary interview in which the suspended employees are allowed to explain what happened and present any mitigating circumstances.

It is important to investigate and discuss thoroughly to see if anything led up to the fracas, e.g. recent demotion of one of the participants; ill health (perhaps pre-menstrual tension); the pressure of prosecution delays; bad feeling caused by relationships outside work.

Important factors to consider when deciding whether the reason is sufficiently serious, given all the surrounding circumstances, for the employer to dismiss, may include such matters as was it really a bad fight; in a dangerous situation near to machinery or chemicals; between parties of unequal status, e.g. labourer and company director? Do any of the people involved have a previous history of violence and have they been warned before about violent conduct?

Don't forget to take a look at any written company rules to see what they say about the matter and make sure that in the past there has been consistent treatment of this kind of incident.

Finally, to what degree was the assailant provoked by other people, by abusive remarks, etc. Such a background may give a totally different feel to the situation. Instead of 'you were fighting, that is gross misconduct and you will be dismissed', there may be quite genuine reasons for the employer to consider a lesser penalty than dismissal, e.g. final written warning, disciplinary suspension, transfer or demotion, because of the extenuating circumstances. Adjourn the interview so that proper consideration can be given to the decision and, when reconvening the meeting, inform the employees separately of the conclusions reached. Don't forget to tell them about the appeal procedures. Make sure the dismissal is confirmed in writing.

Other Problems

Company Romances

The starting of affairs between company employees, and very often their ending, can cause considerable problems. The Managing Director's secretary having an affair with another senior manager may give rise to fears of leaked confidential information. At the height of an affair the employer may be losing many hours work because the two are 'going into town to get the typewriter ribbons' or disappearing into cupboards and other empty rooms on the sly. This does happen but, as a recent report suggests, most employees in this situation actually do more work and accentuate their compliance with company standards of behaviour even more than they ever did before. Other tensions may be created with the rest of the employees who may resent or be morally affronted by this behaviour, not to mention the loss of their time whilst they gossip about it.

It is not for the employer to take a moral stand on the issue; his only concern should be if the relationship is having a bad effect on the work that goes on in the company. If their relationship spills over into the work situation then he has a perfect right to take disciplinary action. Possibly there are exceptions to this general approach and those would be where, for instance, the organisation is a religious one where such conduct between married persons could be considered as being at variance with the ethos of the organisation and so may justify dismissal.

Consequently, the first line manager must decide whether there is anything that either person should be disciplined for. Loss of time, improper use of storage cupboards, etc., would form grounds for disciplinary action in the usual manner. Breach of confidence in a secretary could be grounds for dismissal if any evidence can be found to support it. A warning beforehand about possible leaks would be even better support for the employer's defence. More often the type of action taken is in the form of warning them not to let the affair spill over into the work situation; to 'cool it' and let the gossip die down. Both people should be informally interviewed, separately, and the employer's concern stated to them. If there is a situation brewing with other staff who may be refusing to work with them, then you should explain that they should play things tactfully.

As with any situation where other employees are trying to pressurise the employer to dismiss, the employer should resist such pressure. Call a meeting and roundly tell them that it is none of their business and that you will only become interested in the star crossed lovers if they allow this relationship to badly affect their work. Alternatively, call in influential employees one at a time and put the matter to them discreetly. However, if this pressure persists you may have to consider dismissing one or both of the employees to restore harmony. You should warn both the employees that this could happen and you would then be obliged to dismiss one or both of them. In practice, this situation almost always resolves itself by one of the persons involved moving off to another company or the whole matter cooling down. Although these discussions are informally arranged, an outline of the discussion should be recorded in a letter to the employees involved, in case the situation deteriorates at a later stage.

Employees with a Body Odour Problem

After this problem has been brought to your attention you should not ignore it and hope it will sort itself out. An employee who smells offensively will be shunned by others and become isolated. Other employees may become very upset if they work in close proximity and could refuse to work alongside them. If the job involves contact with the public or the preparation and handling of food, it is a very undesirable characteristic.

This sort of problem is usually handed over to the personnel officer but there is no reason why it should not be dealt with by the first line manager. Indeed, the situation may eventually require formal disciplinary action to be taken and it is appropriate that the employee's supervisor should inititate action.

All the usual steps should be taken to interview the employee privately and without interruption (see page 29). How do you tell someone they smell? From practical experience, the best way is to be brief, direct and to the point; initially treat it as though you spend most of your time speaking to people about these problems. Look at the person, because looking down at your hands or away into the distance will simply offend. Try to keep a soft tone to your voice as nurses often do.

You could use a formula of words like this: "Thank you for coming to the office. I wanted to have a quiet word with you about your personal hygiene. It is apparent that you are not really taking quite enough care of yourself and I wanted to talk to you to find out why and if there is anything I could do to help. Of course, I hope we can it discuss it now".

Now is the time to use a few settling down tactics like offering a cigarette or a cup of tea. Apart from the expression of surprise and discomfort, I doubt that in most cases an employee — male or female — would respond badly to such an approach. You will, of course, find it necessary to listen to the often embarrassed attempt to explain but the real purpose of the interview is to carry it forward and see what the real problem is.

Sometimes the body odour problem arises from not having enough changes of clothing — just one stinking pin stripe suit that could stand up and walk itself to work. After a person has been unemployed for a period a deterioration of dress is quite noticeable simply because there are not enough funds to replace clothes or to get them cleaned. An advance of salary or wages specifically to buy clothes would help. Men often need to be encouraged to buy new new shoes to help solve the smelly feet problem (some personnel officers think 'odour eaters' should be part of the company's safety equipment!!). There are, of course, other creative solutions to this problem.

Sometimes it is the lack of hot running water, inadequate bath facilities, and housing standards that prevent a reasonable level of cleanliness and that should not be beyond someone's wit to solve.

With younger people it is often the failure to have a hygiene routine, i.e. wash every day, stripwashing/bathing at least once a week and regular clean underclothes. Consequently, a little time might be spent comparing routines so that they catch on to what is the norm. Don't forget to mention the use of deodorants and talc.

Another aspect might be explored and that is the fact that the odour is their normal if rather overactive smell — it may be a medical problem, and the employee may already be having treatment for the problem from their doctor. If not, suggest they go to see him.

Most frequently the problem is associated with bereavement, depression or alcoholism and not only do they smell they also generally neglect themselves. Apart from a general pep talk and encouragement to join a social club, get their hair done, dry out, or buy something new to perk themselves up, etc., it is doubtful that very much can be done. Probably encouragement to go to see their doctor is the most constructive thing you can do.

Very often employees don't realise that they have become rather stale and are relieved to have been told. Almost without exception they will make the initial effort. You should stress that it is an important matter and they must pay special attention to it in the future.

If the standard drops off again and there are complaints then there is no reason why the employee cannot be given a first written warning after a disciplinary interview. It is a perfectly reasonable request for the employer to make and to expect the employee to comply with. Consequently it is an area where the employer can apply the disciplinary procedure, even to ultimately dismissing the employee.

Misconduct Away from Work

The off duty conduct of an employee may cause the employer to consider the dismissal of an employee because the conduct has an unfavourable effect on his company. In most cases, such conduct should not be the concern of the employer unless he can show that it is relevant to the position of trust the employee holds, affects his integrity or affects the working relationship with other staff or customers. Sometimes it is made clear in company rules that conviction of a serious offence will lead to dismissal. Additionally, professional codes of conduct may affect the employee's continued ability to practice his profession if convicted of a serious offence.

An industrial tribunal will also check that the employer investigated properly. Often information of the incident arrives second hand from another employee or the newspaper. Check that it is the right Mr. J. Smith of High Street, Dorking, before plunging in. What precisely was the charge and what was the final verdict? Does it mean a period of imprisonment and if so for how long can you keep the job open, bearing in mind the job has to be done in the meantime? All these questions must be answered in an interview with the employee if it is at all possible. Sometimes it will be necessary to talk to the employee's solicitor to get this information if he has gone to gaol. Once you have this information you are in a position to decide whether or not to retain the employee. Any dismissal like this, which is not related to misconduct at work, should be effected with notice being given.

Where an employee has been convicted of a serious or violent crime, other employees might feel genuinely concerned about working with the employee again. Once again it depends on the job. If it is a responsible one supervising young immature staff it might be justifiable to dismiss, but do consider transfer to another job where such responsibilities don't exist. If the offence is not really relevant to the job then resist any pressure by other employees to dismiss, certainly at the initial stages. If that doesn't do the trick, then in order to restore harmony it may become necessary to dismiss. If that situation is likely to arise, warn the employee and confirm in writing afterwards that if relationships with other staff become intolerable he will have to go.

If it is a question of not trusting an employee because she holds the position of cashier and she has been convicted of shop lifting at another store, this could form reasonable grounds for dismissal, but do consider if it is feasible to transfer her to other work that does not involve a position of trust and access to money or goods.

If the employee's name is blazoned across the local paper for some very colourful behaviour it may form grounds for dismissal if it affects the employer's reputation but this is a difficult area and probably better ignored when it has no bearing on the job. What is news today is quickly forgotten tomorrow.

Summary

No one would ever claim that the disciplinary aspects of the supervisor's or manager's job are easy; however, we hope that, in the preceding pages, we have shown that by using well-defined routines much of the heat can be taken out of the situation.

So long as the problem is approached in a constructive manner, with the aim being to get the employee back on to the right track and not to get him out of the door, and this approach is recognised by the workforce as a whole, then the difficulties of maintaining order will be considerably reduced.

To summarise the procedures that should normally be followed, the stages are:

- what is the problem? Gather together the facts — including precise details of the standards that should have been reached; ensure that there really is a problem and decide what standard the employee should be achieving;

- should the employee have been aware that his behaviour was out of line with the standards? Consider here whether there was a written rule, whether the employee should have been aware of it, and whether the rule has been enforced;

- give the employee a chance to give his side of the story; ensure you can speak privately, encourage a two-way conversation; consider the employee's replies and, if necessary, adjourn the meeting while you consider any new facts;

- check on your company's own procedure to see what the next appropriate stage is if you are not satisfied with the employee's replies: should you be giving an informal, formal, oral or written warning, or passing the matter on to the next management level?;

- whatever disciplinary action is taken ensure first that it is appropriate — that "the punishment fits the crime" and, as far as possible, that it will have a positive effect in encouraging the employee to mend his ways; ensure that the employee understands why you are taking the action;

- consider what effect your action will have on other employees; if a previously lax standard of discipline is being tightened up, a general warning to all relevant employees is usually better initially than making an example of one transgressor;

- if the warning is to be in writing, ensure that it details, in specific terms wherever possible, what improvement you expect, within what period of time, and the consequences if the improvement is not made, is insufficient, or is not maintained;

- monitor the employee's behaviour — constructively — throughout the review procedure; no further formal action should be taken during this period unless it becomes absolutely clear that no improvement will be forthcoming or some other serious misconduct arises.

Periodic Review

Over time, standards of behaviour expected from employees change, as do standards of work, dress, and so on. Similarly changes in the law may occur or your own industrial relations practice may change. To ensure that your disciplinary rules and procedures reflect these changes and so do not fall into disuse or become irrelevant, they should be subject to regular review.

Where recognised trade unions are involved they should be consulted on the changes made and they, and all of the workforce, should be clearly told the reasons for any changes so that suspicions don't arise that you are using the procedures to edge out employees without redundancy payments.

If the rules or procedures form part of the contract, then, in theory at least, you need the consent of the workforce as it is not open to employers to vary contracts unilaterally. This consent is essential in any event since rules are only workable in general if there is a broad concensus in favour of (or at least not directly opposed to) their objectives.

Index

Absenteeism...70
ACAS Code of Practice 7
Accepting warnings 45
Action short of dismissal.............................54
Alcoholism...64
Appeals..47

Body odour 83
Breach of contract..13

Calling disciplinary meetings.....................56
Checklists
      dismissal after warnings 62
      dismissal for gross misconduct 63
      formal disciplinary interviews.............60
      informal disciplinary interviews 37
      when to take formal action 39
      whether action should be taken 26
Code of practice on discipline 7
Common law 13
Company romances......................................81
Company rules, codifying 3
Consistency...23
Constructive dismissal 14
Contracts of employment 13

Demotion 54
Disciplinary interviews
      hints on conducting 30
      monitoring the success of 36
      organisation of 29
      preliminary tactics 27
      problem areas 33

Disciplinary procedures
     essential features of...7
     operation of...43
Disciplinary rules 10
Discipline, definition of...1
Dismissal
     fair reasons for 6
     without warning..63
     written reasons for...63
Documentation 31
Drunkenness 64

Employees with B.O..83
Example procedure for non-unionised company 40
Excuses, assessment of 32

Fact finding 23
Fighting 52, 80
Final warnings..62
Formal interviews..55, 60
Formal procedures..39

Giving written warnings..44
Grievance procedures 47
Gross misconduct..49
     dismissal for...63
     fighting..80
     theft...78

Industrial tribunals...6
     role of the supervisor/manager....................................9
Informal interviews...27, 37
Informal warnings 25
Interviewing employees 27
Investigation 57

Job performance...75

Keeping to the procedure 40

Lateness 65
Life span of warnings 46

Minor misconduct 65
Minutes of meetings...56
Misconduct outside work 85
Monitoring the success of interviews 36

Non-union company procedure 40
Notice of dismissal..55

Office romances..81

Periodic reviews..88
Physical assault...80
Poor performance 75
Preliminary tactics in interviews....................................27
Procedures for dealing with
        absenteeism..70
        body odour..83
        fighting..80
        job performance 75
        lateness 65
        misconduct outside work....................................85
        office romances 81
        theft..78

Reasons for dismissal in writing 63
Reprimands..25
Responsibilities of supervisors/managers 24
Review periods..48
Reviewing rules and procedures.....................................88
Right to be accompanied at disciplinary meetings..............44
Right to explain 79
Role at tribunal...9

Romances between employees 81
Rules, sample of 10

Shop stewards 34
    taking disciplinary action against 58
Sick pay 71
Solicitors 35
Summary dismissal 49
Suspending employees 51
    legal aspects 14

Tape recording interviews 56
Terminating employment 55
Theft 78
Timekeeping 65
Totting up warnings 43
Trade unions, role in disciplinary procedures 16, 34
Transfers 54

Unfair dismissal 5
Union representatives 34

Warning letters
    absence 72
    poor performance 76
    timekeeping 68
Welfare concerns 22
Witnesses 52, 56
Written reasons for dismissal 63
Written rules and procedures 9
Written warnings 44
    how to give them 59
    life span of 46